THE
SECRET
GARDEN

THE SECRET GARDEN

MUSICAL BOOK AND LYRICS BY

Marsha Norman

MUSIC BY

Lucy Simon

BASED ON THE NOVEL BY

Frances Hodgson Burnett

THEATRE

COMMUNICATIONS

GROUP

TCG gratefully acknowledges public funds from the National Endowment for the Arts, the New York State Council on the Arts and the New York City Department of Cultural Affairs in addition to the generous support of the following foundations and corporations: Alcoa Foundation, Ameritech Foundation, ARCO Foundation, AT&T Foundation, Citibank N.A., Consolidated Edison Company of New York, Council of Literary Magazines and Presses, Nathan Cummings Foundation, Dayton Hudson Foundation, Exxon Corporation, Ford Foundation, GTE, James Irvine Foundation, Jerome Foundation, Management Consultants for the Arts, Andrew W. Mellon Foundation, Metropolitan Life Foundation, National Broadcasting Company, Pew Charitable Trusts, Philip Morris Companies Inc., Scherman Foundation, Shubert Foundation, L. J. Skaggs and Mary C. Skaggs Foundation, Lila Wallace-Reader's Digest Fund.

Cover logo art by Doug Johnson

Norman, Marsha.
The secret garden : book and lyrics / by Marsha Norman. — 1st ed.
Adaptation from : The secret garden / by Frances Hodgson Burnett.

Design and composition by The Sarabande Press

For Angus and Katherine,
North, Nash and Dodge,
Julie and James

ACKNOWLEDGMENTS

For her inspired vision, her courage, and her vigilance
as producer, set designer and friend,
the authors wish to thank
Heidi Landesman.

The Secret Garden opened on Broadway at the St. James Theatre on April 25, 1991. It was produced by Heidi Landesman, Rick Steiner, Frederic H. Mayerson, Elizabeth Williams, Jujamcyn Theaters/TV ASAHI and Dodger Productions. Scenery was by Heidi Landesman, costumes by Theoni V. Aldredge, lighting by Tharon Musser, choreography by Michael Lichtefeld, musical direction by Michael Kosarin and direction by Susan H. Schulman. The cast was as follows:

LILY	Rebecca Luker
MARY LENNOX	Daisy Eagan

In Colonial India:

FAKIR	Peter Marinos
AYAH	Patricia Phillips
ROSE LENNOX	Kay Walbye
CAPTAIN ALBERT LENNOX	Michael De Vries
LIEUTENANT WRIGHT	Drew Taylor
LIEUTENANT SHAW	Paul Jackel
MAJOR HOLMES	Peter Samuel
CLAIRE HOLMES	Rebecca Judd
ALICE	Nancy Johnston

At Misselthwaite Manor:

ARCHIBALD CRAVEN	Mandy Patinkin
DR. NEVILLE CRAVEN	Robert Westenberg
MRS. MEDLOCK	Barbara Rosenblat
MARTHA	Alison Fraser
DICKON	John Cameron Mitchell
BEN	Tom Toner
COLIN	John Babcock
JANE	Teresa De Zarn
WILLIAM	Frank DiPasquale
NURSE	Betsy Friday
TIMOTHY	Alec Timerman
MRS. WINTHROP	Nancy Johnston

The Secret Garden was originally produced by Virginia Stage Company in 1989. R. J. Cutler directed.

CHARACTERS

LILY, Mary's aunt, Mr. Craven's wife, now dead.

MARY LENNOX, a ten-year-old girl.

MRS. MEDLOCK, Mr. Craven's housekeeper.

DR. NEVILLE CRAVEN, Mr. Craven's brother.

MARTHA, a housemaid.

ARCHIBALD CRAVEN, Mary's uncle, and lord of Misselthwaite Manor.

BEN WEATHERSTAFF, head gardener.

DICKON, Martha's brother.

COLIN CRAVEN, Mr. Craven's ten-year-old son.

MRS. WINTHROP, headmistress.

MAJOR SHELLEY

MRS. SHELLEY

SERVANTS

DREAMERS:

ROSE LENNOX, Mary's mother.

CAPTAIN ALBERT LENNOX, Mary's father.

ALICE, Rose's friend.

LIEUTENANT WRIGHT, officer in Mary's father's unit.

LIEUTENANT SHAW, fellow officer.

MAJOR HOLMES

CLAIRE HOLMES, his wife.

FAKIR

AYAH, Mary's Indian nanny.

The characters referred to collectively as the Dreamers are people from Mary's life in India, who haunt her until she finds her new life in the course of this story. They are free to sing directly to us, appearing and disappearing at will.

PLACE

Colonial India, and Misselthwaite Manor, North Yorkshire, England.

TIME

1906.

ACT I

PROLOGUE

Behind a scrim, a beautiful young woman, dressed in white, sits sus-
pended high over the stage in a Victorian oval picture frame. A small girl
named Mary is seated downstage playing with an elaborate dolls' house.
As Lily, the young woman, sings, Mary hums.

LILY:

> Clusters of crocus,
> Purple and gold,
> Blankets of pansies,
> Up from the cold.
> Lilies and iris,
> Safe from the chill,
> Safe in my garden,
> Snowdrops so still.

An Indian Fakir appears and begins to chant.

FAKIR:

> Ah . . .
> A'o jadu ke mausam.
> A'o garmiyo ke din.
> A'o mantra tantra yantra
> Us ki bimari hata 'o.

3

Ah . . .
A'o jadu ke mausam.
A'o garmiyo ke din.
A'o mantra tantra yantra
Us ki bimari hata 'o.

English couples appear, as if in a dream. They are at the end of a dinner party. Those present include: Rose, Mary's mother, a beautiful woman who seems to be flirting with all the men. Albert, Mary's father. Alice, Rose's friend. Two lieutenants, Wright and Shaw, serving the Raj in colonial India. Major Holmes and his wife, Claire. The Fakir, and Mary's Ayah. At Albert's salute, the Dreamers begin to play "Drop the Handkerchief" using a red handkerchief. Mary wanders through the party.

The echo of children's voices is heard.

CHILDREN'S VOICES:
    Mistress Mary, quite contrary,
    How does your garden grow?
    Not so well, she said, see the lily's dead,
    Pull it up, and out you go.

As the game proceeds, we realize that players are not merely eliminated from the game, but are, in fact, dying of the cholera in colonial India.

CHILDREN'S VOICES:
    Mistress Mary, quite contrary,
    How does your garden grow?
    Far too hot, she cried, see my rose has died,
    Dig it up, and out you go.

4

Look around, look around, what do you see?
Plants in the ground, all are blind to thee.
Walk around, walk around, where will you go?
Seeds in the earth, covered up with snow.

Mistress Mary, quite contrary,
How does your garden grow?
Oh it's dry, she wailed, see the iris failed,
Pull it up, and out you go.

Mistress Mary, quite contrary,
How does your garden grow?
Had an early frost, now it's gone, it's lost.
Dig it up, you're out, you're up, you're out,
You're up, you're out, you go . . .

Finally, no one is left alive, and a mosquito netting falls down over the Dreamers and they disappear.

INDIA

Mary sits on her bed. She has awakened from her dream, and is looking at a small photograph in a frame, and humming "Clusters of Crocus." In the room is the large Victorian dolls' house.

Lieutenant Wright enters, his mouth covered with a handkerchief. He hears the humming and discovers Mary.

LIEUTENANT WRIGHT (*Calling to someone offstage*): Major. There's a girl in here.
MAJOR HOLMES (*As he enters*): Do you mean alive?

MARY: My name is Mary Lennox. Where has everyone gone?
Where's my Ayah?

The Major takes note of the girl, then looks around the room, careful of what he touches, as though everything might be contaminated.

LIEUTENANT WRIGHT: We've searched the servants' bungalow as
well, sir. It's just one blacksnake and this girl.

MARY: Why has no one come for me?

MAJOR HOLMES: I'm afraid there's no one left, Miss.

LIEUTENANT WRIGHT: Bloody miracle she escaped it, though
God knows how. She was drinkin' the same water they was.

MARY: But where are my mother and father?

MAJOR HOLMES: I'm sorry, Miss.

LIEUTENANT WRIGHT: Where shall I take the girl, sir? Our
orders are to burn anything that might be contaminated.

MAJOR HOLMES: To the Governor's house for now, till we find
some family somewhere.

LIEUTENANT WRIGHT: Yes, sir. You'll have to leave that picture
here, Miss.

MARY: No, I will not! I'm taking it with me.

LIEUTENANT WRIGHT: It's your pretty mother, is it?

MARY: No, it isn't.

LIEUTENANT WRIGHT: Yes, well. Come along then.

Mary takes the small framed photo and puts it in her pocket. As they leave the room, the ornate dolls' house bursts into flames.

Lieutenant Shaw appears and sings.

LIEUTENANT SHAW:
Can it be a dream?

Surely it must seem
Like a frightful dream.
How can this be true?

LIEUTENANT WRIGHT AND MAJOR HOLMES:
Won't her mother come?
Come, wake her up to play?
Won't her father say
Here's a rose for you?

CLAIRE, ALICE, HOLMES AND WRIGHT:
There's a girl whom no one sees,
There's a girl who's left alone.
There's a heart that beats in silence
For the life she's never known.
For the life she's never known.

THE LIBRARY AT MISSELTHWAITE MANOR

Mary's uncle, Archibald, his younger brother, Dr. Neville Craven, and the housekeeper, Mrs. Medlock, confer in the library. Dr. Craven holds a telegram.

DR. CRAVEN: Sorry to call you home like this, Archie, but I felt sure you'd want to respond quickly. Here it is. It's from the Governor's office in Bombay. (*Scanning the telegram*) "We regret to inform you that Captain Albert Lennox and his wife Rose have died of the cholera. . . . All in compound perished save their daughter Mary." (*He looks up*) They're asking if they can send the girl here. It seems they found an old will naming you as Mary's guardian.

ARCHIBALD: This is no house for a child.

DR. CRAVEN: I couldn't agree more. Well, we shall simply have to find a boarding school that will take her mid term.

MRS. MEDLOCK: Quite right, sir. There's a convent school not twenty mile away. They'd be quite willing to—

ARCHIBALD: To have her fill the laundry tubs day and night? Thank you, Mrs. Medlock, but the girl is Lily's niece. She will come here.

DR. CRAVEN: She doesn't have to come here, Archie. We can simply locate an appropriate school and they can send her there directly.

Lily and Rose, wearing white lace dresses, enter and play happily, in the past.

ARCHIBALD: Do you remember how Lily and Rose would run 'cross the moor as girls, their lace dresses blowing in the wind?

DR. CRAVEN: But what will she have to do here, Archie? Wander the halls?

MRS. MEDLOCK: We could engage a governess, doctor. That would at least provide her with lessons, and someone to look after her.

DR. CRAVEN: She needs the company of other children, Medlock. Particularly after a tragedy such as this.

They stare at Archibald, who seems to be lost in a reverie. The two girls stop their chase for a moment to talk.

ROSE: Not the gloomy one! Lily, you can't be serious!

LILY: He's only sad, Rose, sad for being alone so long. Archie has the tenderest heart I've ever known.

ARCHIBALD: No. Let our young Mary come here to mourn her loss. And when she has recovered, then we will decide what is best for her. Give me the wire. I'll make the arrangements myself.

Craven hands him the wire and Archibald leaves the room.

ROSE: Silly Lily. Have you been so busy looking into his eyes, that you've missed the hump on his back?

MRS. MEDLOCK: Shall I prepare the girl's room then, doctor?

DR. CRAVEN: It's the worst thing my brother could possibly do for the child.

Archibald reenters.

ARCHIBALD: And Mrs. Medlock, order the child some clothes. I won't have her dressed in black, wandering about like a lost soul. That would make the house even sadder than it is.

MRS. MEDLOCK: Yes, sir.

ARCHIBALD: And you will go to London to meet her and bring her here?

MRS. MEDLOCK: Yes, sir.

ARCHIBALD: Good, then.

Lily and Rose run off together.

ALBERT:
There's a girl whom no one sees,
There's a girl who sleeps alone.

ALBERT, CLAIRE, ALICE, HOLMES, WRIGHT AND SHAW:
There's a heart that beats in silence for
The life she's never known.

A TRAIN PLATFORM IN YORKSHIRE

Major Shelley and his wife arrive with Mary.

MRS. SHELLEY: She's such a sour young thing. Perhaps if Rose had spent more time in the nursery, Mary might have learned some of her mother's pretty ways.

MAJOR SHELLEY: Still. What a nightmare it must have been for the girl. . . . To wander up to bed in the middle of a party, then wake up the next morning with them all dead.

Mrs. Medlock approaches.

MRS. MEDLOCK: Good evening, major. I'm Mr. Craven's housekeeper. Is this the girl?

Rose appears.

MAJOR SHELLEY: Yes ma'am. And here's her papers and the death certificates and all. Her father was captain in my regiment and a fine man he was, too. We're all very sorry . . .

Albert appears.

MRS. MEDLOCK: Thank you, major.

MAJOR HOLMES: Yes ma'am. A pleasant journey to you, ma'am.

Mrs. Medlock turns to Mary.

MRS. MEDLOCK: Well, now. I suppose you'd like to know something about where you are going.

MARY: Would I.

MRS. MEDLOCK: But don't you care about your new home?

MARY: It doesn't matter whether I care or not.

MRS. MEDLOCK: Now in all my years, I've never seen a child sit so still or look so old.

DREAMERS:

High on a hill sits a big old house
With something wrong inside it.
Spirits haunt the halls
And make no effort now to hide it.

What will put their souls to rest
And stop their ceaseless sighing?
Why do they call out children's names
And speak of one who's crying?

MRS. MEDLOCK: Well, you're right not to care. Why you're being brought to Misselthwaite I'll never know. Your uncle isn't going to trouble himself about you, that's sure and certain. He never troubles himself about anyone.

DREAMERS:

And the master hears the whispers
    On the stairways dark and still,
And the spirits speak of secrets
    In the house upon the hill.

MRS. MEDLOCK: He's a hunchback, you see. And a sour young man he was, and got no good of all his money and big place till he were married.

Lily appears in a shaft of light.

MARY: To my mother's sister?

MRS. MEDLOCK: Her name was Lily. And she was a sweet, pretty thing and he'd have walked the world over to get her a blade of grass that she wanted. Nobody thought she'd marry him, but marry him she did, and it wasn't for his money either. But then when she died . . .

MARY: How did she die?

MRS. MEDLOCK: It made him worse than ever. He travels most of the time now. So you needn't expect to see him, because ten to one you won't.

DREAMERS:
High on a hill sits a big old house
With something wrong inside it.
Someone died and someone's left
Alone and can't abide it.

There in the house is a lonely man
Still haunted by her beauty,
Asking what a life can be
Where naught remains but duty.

MARY: Is it always so ugly here?

MRS. MEDLOCK: It's the moor. Miles and miles of wild land that nothing grows on but heather and gorse and broom, and nothing lives on but wild ponies and sheep.

MARY: What is that awful howling sound?

MRS. MEDLOCK: That's the wind, blowing through the bushes. They call it wuthering, that sound. But look there, that tiny light far across there. That'll be the gate it will.

DREAMERS:
> And the master hears the whispers
>> On the stairways dark and still,
>
> And the spirits speak of secrets
>> In the house upon the hill.

THE DOOR TO MISSELTHWAITE

Mary and Mrs. Medlock are met at the door by Dr. Craven.

MRS. MEDLOCK: Mary Lennox, this is Dr. Craven, your uncle's
brother.
MARY: How do you do.
DR. CRAVEN *(To Mrs. Medlock)*: You're to take her to her room.
He doesn't want to see her.
MRS. MEDLOCK: Very good, doctor.

*Mary and Mrs. Medlock go into the house and up the stairs, as the
Dreamers sing their ominous refrain.*

MAJOR HOLMES AND CLAIRE:
> Can it be a dream?
> Surely it does seem
> Like a frightful dream,
> No one here she knows.

ALICE, LIEUTENANTS WRIGHT AND SHAW:
> Portraits on the walls,
> Dark and drafty halls,
> Catch her if she falls,
> Still no fear she shows.

MARY'S ROOM

MRS. MEDLOCK: Well, here you are. This room and the next are where you'll live. But you mustn't expect that there will be people to talk to you. You'll have to play about and look after yourself. But when you're in the house, don't go wandering the halls. Your uncle won't have it.

MARY (*As though asleep or in shock*): . . . won't have it.

Rose and Albert appear.

ROSE: Albert, please . . .

ALBERT: Rose, you and Mary must leave the city until we get this cholera under control.

ROSE: And what shall I do? Wander around the hills, alone with our child, while she stares at me the whole time.

ALBERT: She's not staring at you, Rose. Mary just wants to look at you. Just like all the rest of us.

Mrs. Medlock goes to the door.

MRS. MEDLOCK: Good night, then.

MARY: Yes, ma'am.

Mrs. Medlock lights a candle and exits.

ALBERT (LILY):
There's a girl whom no one sees,
There's a girl who sleeps alone.
There's a heart that beats in silence for
The life she's never known. (Ooo . . .)

Albert extends his arm to Lily, as if asking her to take care of Mary.

But Mary can't sleep. She hears someone crying, picks up a candle and walks out into the house. As she sings, she sees someone rounding a corner and follows him. As she moves through the corridors, she continues to get glimpses of shadows, or ghosts from her past.

Lily follows her.

MARY (LILY):
(Ooo . . .)
I heard someone crying,
Who tho' could it be?
Maybe it was Mother
Calling out, come see.
Maybe it was Father
All alone and lost and cold.
I heard someone crying,
Maybe it was me. (Ooo . . .)

Archibald appears in another part of the gallery, holding his candle aloft.

ARCHIBALD:
I heard someone singing,
Who tho' could it be?
Maybe it was Lily
Calling out to me.
Maybe she's not gone
So far away as I've been told.
I heard someone singing,
Maybe it was she.

Now Mary comes out of her hiding place, as Archibald moves into another part of the house.

MARY:

Maybe it was someone I could
Find and have a cup of tea.
Maybe it was someone who
Could bring the tea and come find me.

LILY:

I heard someone crying,
Tho' I can't say who.
Someone in this house
With nothing left to do.
Sounded like a father
Left alone, his love grown cold.
I heard someone crying,
Maybe it was you.

Mary holds her candle up to a large portrait of Lily.

ARCHIBALD AND MARY:

Maybe I was dreaming of a garden
Growing far below.
Maybe I was dreaming of a life that I
Will never know.

Mary, Lily and Archibald sing together.

MARY AND LILY:

I heard someone crying,
Who tho' could it be?
Someone in this house
Whom no one seems to see.

Someone no one seems to hear
Except for me.
I heard someone crying,
Maybe it was he.

ARCHIBALD:
   Lily, where are you, I'm lost without you,
   I can't walk these halls without you.
   Lily, where are you, I need you,
   I have searched the world but you're not there.
   Come and tell me why you
   Brought me home if you're not here, my
   Lily, where are you, I'm lost without you,
   Lily, I am lost without you.

Having never met, Archibald and Mary return to their rooms through the maze of the corridors.

MAJOR HOLMES, LIEUTENANTS WRIGHT AND SHAW:
   I heard someone crying,
   Who else could it be?
   Surely it was Mary,
   Why can no one see . . .

ROSE, CLAIRE AND ALICE:
   Crying for her mother,
   For the life she's never known.

ALBERT:
   So lost, see her lying
   In her room alone.

LILY:

Ooo . . .

Mary and Archibald blow out their candles.

SCENE ONE

MARY'S SITTING ROOM

Martha, a sturdy Yorkshire girl, enters with a breakfast tray, and a skipping rope around her neck. She sings.

MARTHA:
Me mother asked me, lassie,
Tell us what yer lad mun do,
Afore ye give yer dum de dum
De-dum de-dum de—

MARY: Are you my servant?

Mary's Ayah appears.

MARTHA: Well there, Mary Lennox. Me name is Martha. And now tha'rt up, I'll make the bed.
MARY: Aren't you going to dress me first?
MARTHA: Canna' tha' dress thyself, then?
MARY: In India, my Ayah dressed me.
MARTHA: Well then, it'll do tha' good to wait on thysel' a bit.
'Tis fair a wonder grand folks' children don't turn out fair

19

fools, bein' washed and took out to walk like they was
puppies.

MARY: What *is* this language you speak?

MARTHA: Well of course you've not heard any Yorkshire, livin' in
India, have ye. Mrs. Medlock said I'd have to be careful or
you wouldn't understand what I was sayin'. But I didn't know
what to expect from you either, lassie. When I heard you was
comin' from Bombay, I thought you'd be a solid brown, I did.
But you're not brown at all. More yellow, I'd say.

MARY: It's the natives who are brown.

MARTHA: Well, maybe I was hoping you'd be brown, is more the
truth of it. I've never seen a brown person.

*Mary's hands fly up to her eyes, as she bursts into tears and doesn't want
Martha to see it.*

MARTHA: Eh, now lassie, you mustn't cry like that, I didn't
know you'd be so easy vexed. I'll help you on with your
clothes this time, if you like. You just pretend you're back in
India, and I'm your servant, and you just give me that little
yellow foot.

MARY: I'm quite all right. Thank you.

MARTHA: Look there. Out the window. It's the moor it is. Like a
dull purple sea this morning. Do you like it?

MARY: I hate it.

MARTHA: Ah, you wait till spring. For the moor is fair covered
in gorse and heather, and there's such a lot of fresh air. My
brother Dickon goes off and plays on the moor for hours. He's
got a pony that's made friends with him, and birds and sheep
and such as eats right out of his hand.

Mary has been examining the closet.

MARY: Those are not my clothes.

MARTHA: Ay, Miss, your uncle—

MARY (*Interrupting her to keep her from talking on and on*): These are nicer than mine.

Martha hears Mrs. Medlock's bell.

MARTHA: You get these new clothes on then, and wrap up warm and run out and play. That'll give you stomach for your porridge.

MARY: Mrs. Medlock told me there's nothing out there but a big old park.

MARTHA: Well, maybe you'll run into our Dickon out there. Maybe he'll give you a ride on his pony. Maybe he'll—

MARY: I don't know anything about boys.

Martha sighs, and proceeds to dress Mary as she sings.

MARTHA:
If I had a fine white horse
I'd take you for a ride today.
But since I have no fine white horse
Inside I'll have to stay,
    And empty all the chamber pots
    And scrub the floors and such.
But what's there to do on a fine white horse?
It seems to me not much.

If I had a wooden boat
I'd take you for a sail today.
But since I have no wooden boat
Inside I'll have to stay,

And catch and kill the mice
And pluck the chickens for the cook.
But what's there to do on a wooden boat
But sit up straight and look.

And worry our boat will start to drift
And float us out to sea . . .
And land us on an isle of gold,
Oh dear, oh dearie me . . .

If I had a chambermaid,
I'd take you out to play today.
They say out there's a maze where
Once you enter, there you stay.
For certain we'd get lost and they'd
Come lookin' for our bones
And find us sometime late next week
And bring us tea and scones.

But what if there's a clan of
Trolls a campin' 'neath a tree?
Or what if there's a pirates'
Cave? Oh dear, oh dearie me . . .

If I wasn't so afraid,
I'd take you out the door today.
But talking birds and tales of
Fairies keep me scared away.
And yes, I promised not to tell what
Else is there, although . . .

If in the maze you chance to see
A garden guarded by a tree
And meet a bird that speaks to thee . . .
Then come and tell my fine white horse
And me.

Mary is dressed now. The bell rings again.

MARTHA: Oh, now there's Mrs. Medlock's bell, and I've got all this to clean up first. Can you find your way out yourself? It's down the stairs, past the ballroom —
MARY: I'll find it.

Martha picks up the skipping rope.

MARTHA: Mary Lennox. I thought tha' might like to have a skipping rope to play with.

Mary takes the skipping rope and throws it down.

MARTHA: Mary Lennox.

Mary turns back to face her.

MARTHA: Tha' forgot tha' rope.

Mary grabs the rope and exits.

SCENE TWO

❧

THE BALLROOM

*Chandeliers are lighted and elegantly dressed couples enter, waltzing.
Something about them seems like a memory. Archibald stands at the door
to the ballroom, as though remembering this scene. Lily dances alone.*

LILY:

A man who came to my valley,
A man I hardly knew,
A man who came to my garden
Grew to love me.

Archibald moves into the scene as he sings.

ARCHIBALD:

A girl I saw in a valley,
A girl I hardly knew,
A girl at work in a garden
Grew to love me.

Archibald begins to dance now too, the music drawing them together.

LILY:

From the gate, he
Called out so kindly,
"Lass wouldst thou 'low me
Rest here, I've ridden quite far."

ARCHIBALD:

"Share my tea," she
Bade me so gently,
Oatcakes and cream,
Sweet plums in a jar . . .

LILY:

And every day to my garden,
This man, who might he be,
Came bearing baskets of roses,
For he loved me.

ARCHIBALD:

All I own, I'd give—

LILY:

—Just a garden . . .

ARCHIBALD:

All I would ask is never to—

LILY:

—Never to leave . . .

LILY AND ARCHIBALD:

Say you'll have me,

Safe you will keep me,
Where you would lead me . . .
There

ARCHIBALD:
   I would,

LILY AND ARCHIBALD:
   There I would,
   There I would,
   There I would go . . .

   A man (girl) who came to my valley,
   A man (girl) I hardly knew,
   A man (girl) who gave me a garden
   Grew to love me.

They waltz. We cannot help but feel the power of their love.

Suddenly Mary enters. The music stops and Lily disappears.

MARY: Are you my Uncle Archibald?
ARCHIBALD: Who's that?
MARY: It's Mary Lennox, sir. Are you my Uncle Archibald?

He tries to regain his composure.

ARCHIBALD: Yes, I am. Good morning, child.
MARY: Are you going to be my father now?
ARCHIBALD: I am your guardian. Though I am a poor one for
   any child. I offer you—

Mary pulls the photograph she brought with her from India out of her pocket.

MARY: Is this my Aunt Lily, in this picture?

He looks at it quickly, this is hard for him.

ARCHIBALD: Yes it is. Where did you get that?

MARY: It was on my dresser, in India. Maybe Mother put it there. I don't know.

ARCHIBALD: Your mother and my Lily—

She grabs the photo back from him.

ARCHIBALD: Please excuse me. (*He notices her coat*) Who dressed you, child?

MARY: Martha tried to, sir.

ARCHIBALD: Yes, I see. (*He tries to adjust the buttons*) I do hope you'll enjoy the gardens. (*He turns to leave*)

MARY: But I want to know what happens to dead people.

And he stops. Death is a subject he cannot resist.

ARCHIBALD: Yes. Well. Quite natural that you should wonder that. (*A moment*) We bury them. We put their things away, we remember things they said. We . . . talk to them, sometimes . . . in our minds, of course . . .

MARY: Can they hear us?

ARCHIBALD (*Now he seems angry at himself*): And then one morning, when we think we're over them at last, we find ourselves in the ballroom, knowing full well we have been here all night, and we draw the painful conclusion that we have been dancing with them again.

MARY: I don't understand.

ARCHIBALD: Nor will you ever. They're not gone, you see. Just dead.

MARY: Is my Aunt Lily a ghost now?

He stops.

ARCHIBALD: Why, have you heard her?

MARY: I heard someone crying in the house last night. But I don't know anything about ghosts. Is my father a ghost now? Does everyone who dies become a ghost?

ARCHIBALD: They're only a ghost if someone alive is still holding on to them.

MARY: Maybe what I heard was Mother, telling me to be nice so you'll keep me.

Now, perceiving her fear, he attempts to reassure her.

ARCHIBALD: The house is haunted, child. Day and night. But it is yours to live in as long as I am master here. I offer you my deepest sympathies on your arrival.

Then he walks away.

MARY (*When he is gone*): Did my mother have any other family?

SCENE THREE

IN THE MAZE

Ben Weatherstaff, a stooped but spry gardener, is at work. Mary is wandering in the gardens.

BEN *(Singing-speaking)*:
Plant a hedge, cut it back,
Dig a hole, try to fill it.
Plant a rose, tie it back,
Find a mole, try to kill it.

It's a maze, this garden, it's a maze of ways,
Any man can spend his day.
It's a maze, this garden, it's a maze of paths,
But a soul can find the way.

For an old man knows how a year it goes,
How the cold hard ground in the spring comes round,
How the seeds take hold and the ferns unfold,
How an English garden grows.

Mary sings, as she learns to skip rope.

MARY:

Skip, skipped the ladies to the master's gate.
Sip, sipped the ladies while the master ate.
Tip, toed the chambermaid and stole their pearls.
Snip, snipped the gardener and cut off their curls.

Dickon is somewhere in the garden. He is quite aware of Mary, though she doesn't see him.

DICKON:

Come along, love, come fly away, fly along,
Come along, fly away home.
Come along, love, you've come a long way,
You've flown all the day,
Fly away home.

BEN (*Singing-speaking*):

Miss a step, trip and fall,
Miss the path, meet the wall.
Miss the way, miss a turn,
Gettin' lost's how you learn.

It's a maze, this garden, it's a maze of paths
Meant to lead a man astray.
Take a left, and then, turning left again's
How a soul can find the way.

(*Singing*)

For an old man knows how a year it goes,
How the cold hard ground in the spring comes round,
How in time it shows how a garden grows,
How an English garden grows.

How the roses climb,
How sublime the time
When an English garden grows.

THE GREENHOUSE

MARY:

Skip, skipped the ladies to the master's gate.
Sip, sipped the ladies while the master ate.
Tip, toed the chambermaid and stole their pearls.
Snip, snipped the gardener and cut off their curls.

Mary enters the greenhouse carrying her skipping rope.

MARY: Good morning, Ben.

BEN: Back again today, are you? What have you been doin' out there?

MARY: Just wandering around. I don't have anybody to play with and nothing to do.

BEN: Dickon's here. Why don't you go talk to him. I saw him myself not five minutes ago, conjurin' with that stick of his.

MARY: I haven't met Dickon. I'm not sure he even exists. I think you and Martha just made him up.

BEN: Well, then, I'll give you a spade if you want to dig a little hole somewhere.

MARY: A little hole for what?

BEN: You and me are a good bit alike. We're neither of us good-looking, and we're both as sour as we look.

There is a moment.

MARY: I saw that robin again today.

BEN: Well, of course you did. There never was his like for bein'
meddlesome. He's the real head gardener around here. Always
chirpin' at me to come see some bush needs prunin'.

MARY: I know where he lives too. It's that square garden with
the tall hedge all around it, and no door, and that funny tree
growing out over the top of the wall. I think that tree is the
same one my Aunt Lily is sitting in in this picture.

*Mary pulls the photo out to show him. He is so moved by the picture, he
doesn't say anything.*

MARY: Am I right?

BEN: That's the one, Missy. That it is. That was Miss Lily's
garden.

MARY: Her garden? But I want to see it. Can you show me the
door?

BEN: No I can't. When she died, your Uncle Archibald locked
the door, said nobody was ever to go in that garden again,
and buried the key. And now the ivy's grown up over the door
such that I don't even know where it is now.

MARY: But aren't you worried that the garden is all dead with
nobody taking care of it?

BEN: Of course I am. But if I so much as set foot in there—

MARY: Maybe the real reason the robin is chirping at you is he
wants you to climb over his garden wall and work on it.

BEN: Maybe he does, but I can't go losin' my job on the advice
of a bird, now can I. And the same goes for you. If they
catch you lookin' for the key—

MARY: They don't care what I do. My Uncle Archie said—

BEN: Your Uncle Archie is gone most of the time, Missy. So
don't you go pokin' your nose where it's no cause to go. Do
you hear me?

She thinks a moment. The Fakir appears.

MARY: Do you believe in spirits?

BEN: That I do, Missy. Old place like this there's more of them than there are of us. Why do you ask?

MARY: I heard that crying in the house again last night.

BEN: That could well be a spirit you heard. They like a tall ceiling and a long hallway to swoop around in.

MARY: In India, once, I saw a spirit pull a big dead snake right up out of a basket and make him dance.

BEN: Well I saw Dickon thaw a frozen baby finch in his bare hands, *and* tell it where its nest was, *and* teach it how to fly there.

MARY: I can do things too, Ben.

BEN: I'm sure you can, Missy. You just stay away from Miss Lily's garden or you're like to find yourself back on the boat. Or worse.

Mary hears the sound of the robin.

MARY: Good day, Ben.

Mary leaves the greenhouse, led by the sound of the robin.

Dickon is revealed in another part of the garden. He looks above him, as though he has just released a wild bird into the sky.

DICKON *(Sings):*
　　Winter's on the wing,
　　Here's a fine spring morn,
　　Comin' clean through the night
　　Come the May . . . say I

Winter's taking flight,
Sweepin' dark cold air
Out to sea, spring is born.
Comes the day . . . I say.

And you'll be here to see it.
Stand and breathe it all the day.
Stoop and feel it, stop and hear it.
Spring, I say.

And now the sun is climbin' high,
Rising fast, on fire,
Glaring down through the gloom.
Gone the gray, I say.
The sun it spells the doom
Of the winter's reign.
Ice and chill must retire.
Comes the May, say I.

And you'll be here to see it.
Stand and breathe it all the day.
Stoop and feel it, stop and hear it.
Spring, I say.

I say
Be gone, ye howling gales, be off ye frosty morns.
All ye solid streams begin to thaw.
Melt, ye waterfalls, part ye frozen winter walls.
See . . . see now it's starting . . .

And now the mist is liftin' high,
Leavin' bright blue air

Rollin' clear 'cross the moor.
Come the May, say I.
The storm'll soon be by,
Leavin' clear blue sky.
Soon the sun will shine.
Comes the day, say I.

And you'll be here to see it.
Stand and breathe it all the day.
Stoop and feel it, stop and hear it.
Spring, I say.

Mary enters another part of the maze, skipping rather proficiently now, and singing a section of "It's a Maze" on "la." Dickon appears from behind a topiary.

DICKON: Hello there, Mary.

MARY: Who are you?

DICKON: I'm Martha's brother, Dickon. I hope I didn't fright thee.

MARY: But what are you doing here?

DICKON: I did fright thee. I'm sorry.

MARY: But why haven't I seen you before?

DICKON: A body has to move gentle and speak low when wild things is about.

MARY: You mean you're here all the time?

DICKON: Well, if somethin' is sick I take a look at it, sure I do. And find the ponies that wander off and the eggs that roll out of the nests, but look here, me mother's sent you a penny's worth of seeds for your garden.

A robin whistle is heard.

DICKON: There's columbine and poppies by the handful.
MARY: I don't have a garden.
DICKON: But don't you want one?

She isn't sure she wants to talk to him.

DICKON: One of your own, I mean.

His spell is beginning to work on her.

DICKON: Come and look at your seeds, why don't you. Well, if
you don't want 'em, I'll . . .

She approaches him, and he pours the seeds in her hand.

The robin is heard again.

MARY: I want to go in that garden. Where the robin lives.
DICKON: I wasn't sure you'd seen him.
MARY: Seen him? He's done nothing but chirp at me ever since I
got here.

The robin whistles.

DICKON: Well, you have to understand, he's makin' his nest.
And he can't afford to have *you* interferin' if you're not
friendly.

*The robin whistles again. Dickon takes Mary's skipping rope and begins to
play with it.*

MARY: How do you know that?

DICKON: Because we were just talkin' about you, how do you think?

MARY: He was talking too, or just you?

DICKON: What he thinks, is that you're lookin' for a nest yourself, only it looks to him like your nest would have to be pretty big.

MARY: Have you ever been in there?

DICKON: It's not mine to go into, Mary. But it might be yours, I can't say. He's been keepin' it safe for somebody, that much I know.

MARY: He has?

DICKON: Same way as the ivy grown up over the door. But maybe the robin is waitin' to hear why you want to go in there, exactly. Bein' as he's got the safest nestin' spot in all England, he's wise to be wary.

MARY: Can you tell him I'm friendly?

DICKON: I could, but what if you wanted to tell him something else and I wasn't here. Be much quicker if you learned to talk to him yourself.

MARY: But what could I say that he would understand?

DICKON: Well I wouldn't mention you were an egg-eater, if you know what I mean. But are you interested in flyin' perhaps? Or bugs.

MARY: I'm afraid not.

DICKON: Well, then just tell him about yourself, and I'll translate into Yorkshire for you till you get the way of it.

The robin trills.

MARY *(Sings)*:
  I . . .

DICKON:

She . . .

MARY:

I'm a girl . . .

DICKON:

She is a lass
As took a graidley fancy to thee.
Dost tha' fear?

MARY:

Tha' mun not fear . . .

DICKON:

She's took thee on
For like to vex thee.
Nowt o' the soart.

MARY:

Nowt o' the soart.

DICKON:

She knows fair well
She mun not fright thee.

MARY:

Canna' tha' show me . . .

DICKON:

Fair better to know her . . .

MARY:
Show me tha' key.

DICKON:
Show her tha' key.

The robin trills again.

DICKON:
She's a lass and tha' art right
As needs a spot where she can rest in.

MARY:
I mun sit where I'll not be
So thinkin' thoughts or feel a guest in.

DICKON:
Nowt o' the soart,

MARY:
Nowt o' the soart.

DICKON:
She'd fair be watchin' for the spring.

MARY:
I'll not be climbin' up, I'll only be callin' good morning,
And fair low I'll sing.

DICKON: Well done, Mary.

The robin trills again.

Lily and Rose, as young girls, wander into the maze.

ROSE: Lily, what are you looking for?
LILY: Wait till you see it. It's the most beautiful garden I ever
. . . and nobody knows about it except Archie . . . but
I can never find the door, oh wait, maybe it's on this other
side . . .

MARY:
I'll only walk around as like to
    See it for mysel'.
If tha' canst 'low me visit I'll
    Speak low e'en to thysel'.
Tha'll not be bothered night and day
    By wenches racin' round,
I'll but seem a silent dream
    Standin' on the secret ground.

I'd but smell the growin' things,
    Count the roses 'gainst the wall,
Hear thy babes when first they peck,
    Stretch my hand if they should fall.
Or if tha' likes, I'll bring thee seeds
    Or worms all in a mound,
For if tha'll have me for tha' friend
    Tha'll be the first I've found.

I'm a lass,

DICKON:
    A trusty lass,

MARY:

As took a graidley fancy to thee.
Canna' tha' show me . . .

DICKON:

Fair well tha' dost know her . . .

MARY:

Show me tha' key?

MARY AND DICKON:

Show me (her) tha' key.

DICKON: Well. I'm off, then.

MARY: But where are you going?

DICKON: I can't say. But I'll see you tomorrow sure enough. And
if you need me before then, well, now that you and robin is
talking, he always knows where I am.

MARY: But can't you help me look for the key?

DICKON: But that's why I'm leavin', Mary. A body can't find a
thing in a crowd.

MARY: All right, then. Bye.

Dickon stands behind her and sings.

DICKON:

And you'll be here to see it.
Stand and breathe it all the day.
Stoop and feel it, stop and hear it.
Spring . . . I say.

Dickon hangs the skipping rope around one of the topiaries and leaves.

MARTHA (*Calling from offstage*): Mary Lennox!

Mary starts to leave, but the robin stops her with a trill, reminding her, perhaps, to take her skipping rope. Mary pulls the rope from off the topiary, dislodging something.

MARY: Oh, no. Look what I've—

She hears a metallic clink, as something falls into the leaves at her feet.

MARY: What was that?

She bends over to pick it up, brushing away the leaves where it is now buried.

MARY: Where did it . . . (*She finds it*) There it is! It's a key! It's the key to the garden! I found the key to the garden! It was right here! (*Now she remembers*) The door! But where is the door?

She stands holding the key close to her.

MARTHA (*From offstage*): Mary Lennox!
MARY: Coming!

Mary puts the key in her pocket quickly and runs toward the house.

MARTHA (*Enters looking for Mary*): Mary Lennox! We haven't got time to play hide and seek now. Mrs. Medlock wants us in the house, now! Mary!

She exits as the Ayah and Fakir appear.

AYAH AND FAKIR:

Skip, skipped the ladies to the master's gate.
Sip, sipped the ladies while the master ate.
Tip, toed the chambermaid and stole their pearls.
Snip, snipped the gardener and cut off their curls.

SCENE FOUR

ARCHIBALD'S LIBRARY

Archibald enters wearing a heavy raincoat.

ARCHIBALD: Will this rain never stop?

DR. CRAVEN: Archie, we must undertake some work on the house. We simply can't stand by while these storms tear it down, piece by piece. And the same for the grounds.

ARCHIBALD: Actually, I was just standing outside hoping to see the whole place struck by lightning.

DR. CRAVEN: If you have no interest in maintaining the herds and the gardens, then say so, and we'll lease the pastures and fields, and get the estate down to a manageable size.

ARCHIBALD: Will you never stop! Father should've given Misselthwaite to you, Neville, not me.

DR. CRAVEN: You are the elder brother, Archie. That would never have occurred to him. But if you continue to feel you cannot live here, then leave. You were happy once before. In Paris. You're still a young man. There is no reason—

ARCHIBALD: I can't leave, Neville.

DR. CRAVEN: But what good does it do to sit by the boy's bed, night after night, hoping for a miracle.

44

ARCHIBALD: They have been known to happen.

DR. CRAVEN: When Lily died, I gave up my practice to care for the—

ARCHIBALD: You've been completely faithful, Neville. I am deeply grateful.

DR. CRAVEN: But I did not give up my responsibility to *you*, Archie. I cannot let you waste your life waiting for the inevitable end. I cannot.

ARCHIBALD: I am not wasting my life, Neville. This *is* my life now.

Mrs. Medlock enters, with Mary.

MRS. MEDLOCK: Beg pardon, sir, you sent for young Mary.

ARCHIBALD: Yes, child. Come in. Perhaps we can manage to have a moment before the storm carries us away. Take a chair.

She takes a seat.

MARY: Thank you, sir.

And then Archibald realizes he has no idea what he intended to say to Mary.

ARCHIBALD: Are you well? Do they take good care of you?

MARY: Yes, sir. Thank you, sir.

ARCHIBALD: I'm sorry it's been so long since we've spoken. It's just I keep forgetting you. (*Another pause*) I intended to find you a school to go to or—

MARY: Oh no, please don't send me away!

ARCHIBALD: No, of course not. But perhaps you would enjoy a governess, considering that you've had a chance to look around now and know there's nothing for you to do. What do you say to that?

MARY: Please don't make me have a governess, sir. There's everything for me to do here. There are so many gardens to walk around in, and so much to learn about them. Martha gave me a skipping rope, and Dickon gave me some seeds and . . .

Albert appears upstage.

ALBERT: And here's a rose for you, Mary . . .

ARCHIBALD: Yes, all right then . . .

ALBERT: Happy birthday, darling.

ARCHIBALD: Play outside if you like, but is there anything you need? Would you like some toys, or books or dolls perhaps?

MARY: Might I . . .

ARCHIBALD: Speak up, child.

MARY: Might I have a bit of earth, sir?

ARCHIBALD: A bit of earth?

MARY: To plant seeds in. Yes, sir. A garden.

Archibald is clearly moved by this request. This is exactly the way Lily used to talk. Neville is alarmed.

ARCHIBALD: Do you care about gardens so much, then?

MARY: I didn't know about them in India. I was always ill and tired and it was too hot. I sometimes played at making little flower beds, sticking things in the sand. But here, I might have a real garden if you would allow it, sir.

ARCHIBALD: Are you sure there's nothing else?

MARY: No, sir.

ARCHIBALD: Yes, all right, then. You may have your earth. Take as much earth as you want.

MARY: Thank you very much, sir.

He tries to indicate that Mary may leave the room. But she mistakes his gesture for a wave, and waves back.

DR. CRAVEN: You may leave, child.

Mary leaves the room, and after a moment, Archibald turns to Dr. Craven.

ARCHIBALD: It's much worse being back this time. The dreams are much more vivid. And I hear things. In the halls.

DR. CRAVEN: It's the girl, Archie.

ARCHIBALD: Do you mean Mary? But I never see her.

DR. CRAVEN: Because you can't see her, Archie, because she reminds you of Lily.

ARCHIBALD: You can't be serious.

DR. CRAVEN: I can see the resemblance, myself. Although Lily's hair was more . . . . You were very kind to take the girl in, Archie, but in your state, it's simply too much. If you allow the girl to stay here, to grow up here, I have no doubt your dreams, to say the very least, will get even worse.

ARCHIBALD: But you can see the girl is lonely, Neville. Perhaps I should have more conversations with her.

DR. CRAVEN: I don't think that is wise, Archie.

ARCHIBALD: A bit of earth . . .

DR. CRAVEN: Until you are ready to send her to a school . . .

ARCHIBALD *(Begins to sing)*:
She wants a little
Bit of earth,
She'll plant some seeds.

DR. CRAVEN: . . . it is my professional advice that you continue to obey your natural instincts and avoid her.

ARCHIBALD:
  The seeds will grow,

DR. CRAVEN: Archie . . .

ARCHIBALD:
  The flowers bloom,
  But is their bounty
  What she needs?

DR. CRAVEN: If I could have your signature on these leases.

ARCHIBALD:
  How can she chance
  To love a little
  Bit of earth?
  Does she not know?
  The earth is old
  And doesn't care if
  One small girl wants things
  To grow.

  She needs a friend,
  She needs a father,
  Brother, sister,
  Mother's arms.
  She needs to laugh,
  She needs to dance
  And learn to work
  Her girlish charms.

She needs a home.
The only thing
She really needs
I cannot give.
Instead she asks
A bit of earth,
To make it live.

    She should have a pony,
    Gallop 'cross the moor.
    She should have a dolls' house
    With a hundred rooms per floor.
    Why can't she ask for a treasure,
    Something that money can buy,
    That won't die? When
    I'd give her the world,
    She asks, instead,
    For some earth.

A bit of earth,
She wants a little
Bit of earth,
She'll plant some seeds.
The seeds will grow,
The flowers
Bloom, their beauty
Just the thing she needs.

She'll grow to love
The tender
Roses, lilies fair,
The iris tall.

And then in fall,
Her bit of earth
Will freeze and
Kill them all.

A bit of earth, a bit of earth,
A bit of earth, a bit of earth . . .

And with a crash of thunder and a stroke of lightning, the storm hits.

SCENE FIVE

MISSELTHWAITE MANOR
IN THE GALLERY

Large portraits of Lily loom in the air, as the Dreamers circle around
Archibald, and sing.

MAJOR HOLMES:
Close the shutters and lock the doors.

ALBERT:
Brace the windows as in it pours.

FAKIR:
Candles only the ones you carry,

LIEUTENANT SHAW:
Watch now,

LIEUTENANT WRIGHT:
Careful the stairs,

WRIGHT AND SHAW:

Working in pairs,

ALBERT:

Fares well a house that's ready . . .

DREAMER MEN:

Comin' a terrible storm,
Sounds like a train on the rail,
Sky is a dangerous hue,
Full of the thunder and hail.
Not since I was a child, have I
Felt such a fear in the vale.

Thunder and lightning outside the house.

ROSE:

See the ho/rses are free,

ALICE:

Loose their reins.

AYAH:

Tie the carriages fast,

CLAIRE:

Lock the chains.

AYAH AND ALICE:

Call out quickly if lightning strikes the sheds now.

ROSE:
Checking supplies,

AYAH AND CLAIRE:
Watching the skies . . .

DREAMER WOMEN:
Fares well the house that's ready . . .

DREAMERS:
Comin' a terrible storm,
Looks like the sea in a gale,
Branches are broken in half,
Carried aloft like a sail.
Not since I was a child, have I
Heard such a horrible wail.
Ah . . .

There is a lull in the storm, and we find Dr. Craven thinking about the other storm he knows is brewing.

DR. CRAVEN:
Strangely quiet, but now the storm
Simply rests to strike again.
Standing, waiting, I think of her,
I think of her . . .

In another part of the house, Archibald is looking at the portrait of Lily.

ARCHIBALD:
Strange, this Mary, she leaves the room
Yet remains, she lingers on.

Something stirs me to think of her,
I think of her . . .

DR. CRAVEN:

From death she casts her spell,
All night we hear her sighs,
And now a girl has come
Who has her eyes.

She has her eyes,
The girl has Lily's hazel eyes.
Those eyes that saw him happy long ago,
Those eyes that gave him life and hope he'd never known.
How can he see the girl and miss those hazel eyes?

ARCHIBALD:

She has her eyes,
The girl has Lily's hazel eyes.
Those eyes that closed and left me all alone,
Those eyes I feel will never ever let me go.
How can I see this girl who has her hazel eyes?

In Lily's eyes a castle
This house seemed to be,
And I her bravest knight became,
My lady fair was she.

DR. CRAVEN (*So angry and hurt*):

She has her eyes,
She has my Lily's hazel eyes.
Those eyes that loved my brother, never me,
Those eyes that never saw me, never knew I longed

To hold her close, to live at last in Lily's eyes.

ARCHIBALD:
Imagine me, a lover.

DR. CRAVEN:
I longed for the day
She'd turn and see me standing there.

ARCHIBALD AND CRAVEN:
Would God had let her stay.

She has her eyes,
She has my Lily's hazel eyes.
Those eyes that first I loved so long ago.
How can I now forget that once I dared to be
In love, alive and whole in Lily's eyes, in Lily's eyes.

SCENE SIX

THE HALLWAY

Mary enters the gallery, holding a candle. Martha and Lily also wander the gallery.

MARY:
　　Someone is crying, just now I heard them,
　　Someone in this house is crying.
　　Why won't they tell me, I know they're lying.
　　Someone here is lost or mad.
　　I must try to find them,
　　Beg them stop so I can sleep.

　　I heard someone crying,
　　Who tho' could it be?
　　Someone in this house
　　Whom no one seems to see.
　　Someone no one seems to
　　Hear except for me . . .
　　I heard someone crying . . .

MARY AND AYAH:

I heard someone crying . . .

CLAIRE:

I heard someone crying . . .

LIEUTENANT SHAW AND ALICE:

I heard someone . . .

SHAW, WRIGHT, ALICE AND ROSE:

Crying . . .

ALBERT:

I heard someone . . .

FAKIR:

I heard someone . . .

The Dreamers surround Mary, trying to lead her to something or someone. They sing on "ah."

AYAH:

I heard someone crying . . .

ALICE:

Yes, there's someone crying . . .

ROSE:

Someone here is crying . . .

CLAIRE:

Listen, someone's crying . . .

DREAMER WOMEN (MEN):
I heard someone . . . (Ah . . .)
I heard someone . . .

LILY (DREAMERS):
I heard someone . . . (Ah . . .)
Cry . . .

DREAMERS:
Ah . . .

Mary walks through the halls. There is a terrible thunderclap, and the seemingly impenetrable line of Dreamers parts to reveal . . .

SCENE SEVEN

~~~~~~~~~~~~

COLIN'S ROOM

A ghostly form lying on a bed, screaming. Mary is terrified.

COLIN: Get out!

MARY: Who are *you*?

COLIN: Who are *you*? Are you a ghost?

MARY: No I am not. I am Mary Lennox. Mr. Craven is my
uncle.

COLIN: How do I know you're not a ghost?

MARY: I'll pinch you if you like. That will show you how real I
am. Who are you?

COLIN: I am Colin. Mr. Craven is my *father* I see no one and
no one sees me. Including my father. I am going to die.

MARY: How do you know?

COLIN: Because I hear everybody whispering about it. If I live, I
may be a hunchback, but I shan't live.

MARY: Well, I've seen lots of dead people, and you don't look
like any of them.

COLIN: Dead people! Where did you *come* from?

MARY: From India. My parents died there of the cholera. But I

59

don't know what happened to them after that. Perhaps they burned them.

COLIN: My mother died too. When I was born. That's why my father hates me.

MARY: He hates the garden too.

COLIN: What garden?

Mary wishes she hadn't said anything about the garden.

MARY: Just a garden your mother liked. Have you always been in this bed?

COLIN: Sometimes I have been taken to places at the seaside, but I won't stay because people stare at me. And one time a grand doctor came from London, and said to take off this iron thing Dr. Craven made me wear and keep me out in the fresh air. But I hate fresh air, and I won't be taken out.

MARY: If you don't like people to see you, do you want me to go away?

COLIN: Yes, but I want you to come back first thing tomorrow morning and tell me all about India. In the books my father sends me, I've read that elephants can swim. Have you ever seen them swim? They seem too altogether large to be swimmers, unless perhaps they use their ears to—

MARY: I can't come talk to you in the morning. I have to go outside and look for something with Dickon.

COLIN: Who's Dickon?

MARY: He's Martha's brother. He's my friend.

Suddenly, Colin's despotic temperament flares.

COLIN: If you go outside with that Dickon instead of coming here to talk to me, I'll send him away.

MARY: You *can't* send Dickon away!

COLIN: I can do whatever I want. If I were to live, this entire place would belong to me someday. And they *all* know that.

MARY: You little Rajah! If you send Dickon away, I'll never come into this room again.

COLIN: I'll make you. They'll drag you in here.

MARY: I won't even look at you. I'll stare at the floor.

COLIN: You are a selfish thing.

MARY: You're more selfish than I am. You're the most selfish boy I ever saw.

COLIN: I'm selfish because I'm dying.

MARY: You just say that to make people feel sorry for you. If you were a nice boy it might be true, but you're too nasty to die!

Mary turns and stomps away toward the door. The Ayah appears.

COLIN: No, please don't go.

She stops. Her Ayah hums an Indian lullaby.

COLIN: It's just that the storm scares me so that if I went to sleep, I know I'd have such terrible dreams . . .

MARY: But if you keep crying . . .

COLIN: . . . or if I did sleep, I might not wake up.

MARY: Would you like me to stay with you until you fall asleep?

COLIN: I should like that very much.

MARY: Then close your eyes, and I will do what my Ayah used to do in India. I will pat your hand and stroke it and sing something quite low.

COLIN: Do you have bad dreams too?

MARY: Not always. Sometimes I dream about tea parties, but I never know who anybody is at the parties. Or since I've been here, whenever I see my father in a dream, he's a hunchback like your father, and sometimes my Ayah has my mother's face . . .

And without waiting for her to finish, Colin sings.

COLIN:
Some nights I dream
That a round-shouldered man
Comes in my room
On a beam of moonlight.
He never says what he wants,
He just sits with a book in his hands.

And then I dream
That the round-shouldered man
Takes me off on a ride
Through the moors by moonlight.
He never says where we'll go,
We just ride 'cross the hills till dawn.

And some night I'm going to ask him
Is the night sky black or blue.
I know the answer's in his book
Of all that's good and true.

MARY: Maybe your father comes into your room at night and reads while you're asleep . . .

COLIN:
And once I dreamed
That the round-shouldered man

Took my hand and we walked
To a secret garden.
I never knew where we were,
We just sat in the crook of a broken tree.

And some night I'm going to ask him
How the old moon turns to new.
I know the answer's in his book
Of all that's good and true.
I'm sure the answer's in his book
Of all that's good and true.

MARY: Colin, I just realized . . . . We're cousins.

Suddenly, Mrs. Medlock and Dr. Craven enter. Craven goes to the boy.
Mrs. Medlock grabs Mary.

MRS. MEDLOCK: Mary Lennox! You foolish child!

Mrs. Medlock pulls Mary away from the bed.

DR. CRAVEN (*Preparing an injection*): I was afraid of something
like this.
COLIN: No! No! I don't want an—
DR. CRAVEN: He must have his rest. If she's been—
MARY: But I've never seen him before!
DR. CRAVEN: . . . how can I hope to succeed with him if my
orders are not followed.
MRS. MEDLOCK: I've told her to stay in her room, but she refuses
to obey.
COLIN: Get away from me! Don't touch me! No!

Rose appears.

ROSE: Albert!

MARY: I only wanted him to stop crying.

As Dr. Craven wrestles with Colin, Mrs. Medlock takes Mary firmly in hand and walks her to the door.

Albert appears.

ROSE: What *is* that infernal wailing?

ALBERT: It's the servants, Rose.

MRS. MEDLOCK: Now, you listen to me, Mary Lennox.

ALBERT: The cholera. It's quite bad.

LIEUTENANT WRIGHT: Ten thousand dead at last count.

MRS. MEDLOCK: Do you see what you have done?

ALBERT: I should have sent you away while there was still time.

MRS. MEDLOCK: You are *never* to see Colin again.

MARY: But why?

And now other Dreamers appear, as Mary begins to remember exactly what happened at that dinner party.

CLAIRE: It's exactly what they deserve. Letting their sewage run in the streets.

MRS. MEDLOCK: The one rule you were given here you have violated.

LIEUTENANT WRIGHT: But how are we to get around with all the dead in frigging flames?

COLIN: No!

Dr. Craven gives Colin a shot.

ALICE: They're servants, darling. There are millions of them.

MRS. MEDLOCK: Do you want to speak to her, doctor?

DR. CRAVEN: No!

LIEUTENANT SHAW: I wonder if I might have a glass of water.

Colin collapses back on the bed.

MARY: But why didn't you tell me he was here?

ROSE: I'm very warm, Albert.

MRS. MEDLOCK: Because I was ordered not to. And I obey my orders because I want to keep my place here and I advise you to do the same.

ALBERT: Mary! Where is Mary?

MRS. MEDLOCK: Do you understand?

ALBERT: Someone. Find her. There's a child . . .

There is another violent stroke of lightning and Mary runs out of the room and down the hall in absolute terror.

SCENE EIGHT

THE MAZE

Mary rushes outside, and into the maze.

DREAMERS:
　　Comin' a terrible storm,
　　Shakin' the souls of the dead,
　　Quakin' the floor underfoot,
　　Shakin' the roof overhead.
　　Not since I was a child, have I
　　Feared . . .

There is a crash of thunder, and the Dreamers appear, distressed and confused. They cannot help Mary now. They are dying.

Mary runs wildly, trying to find anyone, anything. But the faster she runs, the more terrified she becomes. The Dreamers cannot see her now, she is desperately alone.

ROSE:
　　Mistress Mary, quite contrary,
　　How does your garden grow?

AYAH:

Not so well, she said, see the lily's dead,
Pull it up and out you go.

MAJOR HOLMES:

Mistress Mary, quite contrary,
How does your garden grow?

LIEUTENANT SHAW:

Far too hot, she cried, see my rose has died,
Dig it up and out you go.

ALICE:

Mistress Mary, quite contrary,
How does your garden grow?

CLAIRE:
Oh it's dry, she wailed,
See the iris failed.
Dig it up and out you go.

DREAMERS:
It's a maze this garden,
It's a maze of ways . . .

FAKIR:
Mistress Mary,
Quite contrary,
How does your garden
Grow?

Something wrong
Inside it . . .
It's a maze this garden,
It's a maze of ways . . .

WRIGHT:
Had an early frost
Now it's gone it's lost
Dig it up and out
You go . . .

High on a hill . . .
Something wrong
Inside it . . .

DREAMERS:

It's a maze this garden,
It's a maze of ways
Meant to lead a soul astray.

It's a maze this garden,
It's a maze of ways . . .

It's a maze this garden,
It's a maze of ways
Meant to lead a soul astray . . .

The Dreamers form a circle as in the opening dream. Mary runs round and round it, looking for a way in. In their frenzy the Dreamers sing fragments of songs we have heard before.

CLAIRE:	ALICE:	AYAH:
Mistress Mary	Not since I was	Mah . . .
Mistress Mary	a child	. . .
Mistress Mary	Have I feared	Mistress Mary
Mistress Mary	Have I feared	Mistress Mary

ROSE:	ALBERT:	SHAW:
Crying . . .	For her mother	Mistress Mary
. . .	There's a girl	Mistress Mary
Someone crying	Who no one sees	Mistress Mary
. . .	. . . no one	Mistress Mary

WRIGHT:	FAKIR:	HOLMES:
Skipped the ladies	Ja . . .	Watch now . . .
To the master's gate	Du . . .	Watch now . . .
Skipped the ladies	Ke . . .	Watch now . . .
To the master's gate		

DREAMERS:
Mistress Mary, quite contrary,
How does your garden grow?
Had an early frost, now it's gone, it's lost,
Dig it up and out you go.
You're out, you go!
Out, you go!

Mary looks up and sees her father, the last person alive to think of her. He kneels, opening his arms and heart to her.

ALBERT: Mary! Mary!

She runs into his arms as the other Dreamers disappear from the stage.

As mist fills the stage, Lily appears.

Albert smiles, shows Mary that Lily is waiting for her, and indicates to Mary that she should go with Lily now.

Never looking back, Mary walks to Lily's open arms, and Lily leads Mary up to the garden wall, pulls back the vines, and shows her the door.

Mary wipes her eyes, takes out the key, puts it into the lock and opens the door to the garden.

END OF ACT ONE

ACT II

SCENE ONE

IN THE DREAM GARDEN

A large tea party celebrating Mary's birthday is in progress. Everyone is there, Archibald, Lily, Rose, Albert, Dickon, Martha and the other Dreamers, the living and the dead, exactly the way Mary would like to see them. A photographer stages pictures, a cake is presented, and everyone is serenely happy.

MARY:
   I need a place where I can go,
   Where I can whisper what I know,
   Where I can whisper who I like,
   And where I go to see them.

   I need a place where I can hide,
   Where no one sees my life inside,
   Where I can make my plans, and write them down
   So I can read them.

   A place where I can bid my heart
   Be still, and it will mind me,
   A place where I can go when I am lost—
   And there I'll find me.

I need a place to spend the day,
Where no one says to go or stay,
Where I can take my pen and draw
The girl I mean to be.

*Suddenly, from nowhere, Colin is rolled downstage in his wheelchair by
Mrs. Medlock. Dr. Craven drops a red handkerchief, like the ones in the
cholera dream at the beginning of the show, in his lap. The mood turns
dark and the Dreamers sing.*

LIEUTENANTS WRIGHT AND SHAW:
High on a hill sits a big old house
With something wrong inside it.
Spirits haunt the halls
And make no effort now to hide it.

And the master hears the whispers
    On the stairways dark and still,
And the spirits speak of secrets
    In the house upon the hill.

SCENE TWO

~❧~

ARCHIBALD'S DRESSING ROOM

Dr. Craven comes into Archibald's dressing room. Archibald enters and starts to pack.

DR. CRAVEN: Archie . . . . Archie, you *must* tell me what we are to do with Mary. She goes where she wants to go, and does what she wants to do. I cannot hope to succeed with Colin's treatment if she is allowed to sneak into his room and—

ARCHIBALD: Do you mean he speaks with her?

DR. CRAVEN: The one occasion I witnessed was the worst I've ever seen him. The mere sight of a healthy child threw him into such a rage that I feared he would never recover. If she continues to disturb him, we will have no choice but to put him in hospital.

ARCHIBALD: We will *not* put him in hospital. Lily would never forgive me if I—

DR. CRAVEN: Then you must send her away, before she undoes everything we have tried to do.

ARCHIBALD: I can't send her away, Neville. She has no one on

75

the earth but me. Can't you keep her outside? She likes the gardens, I believe.

DR. CRAVEN: Then *you* take her to the gardens. *You* take on the responsibility of supervising her full-time. She is a strong-willed girl and you are the only one she will obey. What are you doing, Archie?

ARCHIBALD: I'm leaving, Neville. What can I do for Colin when you've made me terrified for him to look at me? And what can I do for Mary if the very sight of the girl sends me into these . . . . You have things well in hand here.

DR. CRAVEN: Well in hand? Haven't you heard anything I've just said?

ARCHIBALD: And last night, I dreamed I walked through the maze to Lily's garden, and saw Lily and Mary standing there. Mary, standing right there in Lily's garden. I turned away . . . I couldn't watch . . . I was afraid . . .

DR. CRAVEN:
Why won't he say what he wants,
Why must he speak in dreams?
Why can't he see what he wants,
To disappear, it seems.

He should send this haunted girl far away,
Leave the house and lands to me . . .

Archibald continues his dream, in song.

ARCHIBALD:
I watched them walk around the garden.
She stood tall, grown strong and bold.

Then they turned, and asked my pardon.
I couldn't speak, my heart grown cold.

DR. CRAVEN:
Why can't he see what he wants?
He wants the past undone.
Why can't he know what he wants—
His losing battles won.

To have never loved her,
Never known how complete a loss can be.

If she could disappear
He'd start again,
And live like other men.
He could be happy then.

If she'd disappear
He could be free,
Cut off from pain and loss,
A bit like me.

Lily and Rose appear.

ROSE: You can't marry this Archibald. He's a gloomy miserable
  cripple who hides himself away in that horrible house. You've
  said it yourself, he can't believe you love him. And neither
  can I!
LILY: No one is asking for your approval, Rose.
ROSE: Lily, if you don't care what happens to you, think about
  your children. Do you want your children to be crippled as
  well?

LILY: I will marry him.

The two debates become a quartet.

DR. CRAVEN:
I can arrange what he wants,
He's left it all to me.
Now he can have what he wants,
Unfettered he will be.
Set him free to wander
Through the world.
Let him go
His lonely way.

ROSE:
Don't do this.
Don't wed him,
Don't bed him,
Don't do this,
Set him free . . .
Through the world.
Let him go
His lonely way.

ARCHIBALD:
And then I longed to join them,
Know the peace they feel,
Their journey done.
Then I woke once more
Without them.
Knew I must wander
    on. And on

LILY:

Now that
I love him,
I will live
For him.
Live just to
    love him.

I
Go
Life to
Find.

ROSE:
I won't forgive you.
Won't see you live
    there.
Lily, I swear
I'll never see you.

DR. CRAVEN:
Just to disappear
Is to be free.

LILY:
Do what you will
Then, I'll

Cut off from pain,
Cut off from pain.

ARCHIBALD:
Cut off from pain,
Cut off from pain.

DR. CRAVEN:
I'll help him

The four sing simultaneously.

DR. CRAVEN:
Disappear.
And start again,
And live like
Other men,
He would be
Happy then.
Just to disappear
Is to be free.
Disappear . . .

ROSE:
Now you must
Leave him.
Yes, you must leave him.
You must believe me,
Lily,
Promise.
Now you must leave him,
You must believe me.

Never leave him.
Cut off from pain.

ROSE:
Cut off from pain,
Cut off from pain.

ARCHIBALD:
Disappear . . .

Leave loss
Behind me.

Live unseen.

Disappear . . .

LILY:
How can I
Leave him?
I'll never leave him,
Nor e'er deceive him.
Rose, I
Promised
Never to leave him.
No, I won't leave him.

Lily, think	I will wed
About the children,	And bear him children.
Lily, think	He will love me,
about the childen.	love the children.

Lily and Rose exit.

ARCHIBALD: I shan't be gone long, perhaps just till the autumn.

DR. CRAVEN: And Mary?

ARCHIBALD: I'll write her a note from Paris.

DR. CRAVEN: You wouldn't be sending Mary away, Archie. Only giving her the education she deserves. I feel quite certain that Albert and Rose wouldn't want the girl to grow up just wandering around.

ARCHIBALD: Yes, I see. Well, then . . . perhaps you should look into a few schools. Someplace she could learn to sing would be pleasant. I leave it all in your hands, Neville. Now, I'll go look in on Colin and—

DR. CRAVEN: Just see that you don't wake him.

ARCHIBALD: In ten years have I ever awakened the boy?

DR. CRAVEN: I'll gather the staff so you can say good-bye.

ARCHIBALD: Oh, for God's sake, Neville. Just let me slip away. (*Then realizing he has been too sharp*) I'm sorry. Tell them . . . (*And then he can't handle it*) Tell them whatever you always tell them.

Archibald leaves and Dr. Craven is left standing there. The Dreamers enter.

ALBERT:
And a man can dream
Of a simple life,

Husband, child and wife,
Love and faith all round.

MAJOR HOLMES:

Then a man must wake,
Stand and greet the day,
See what comes his way,
Feet upon the ground.

ALICE AND CLAIRE:

There's a man whom no one sees,
There's a man who lives alone.
There's a heart that beats in silence for
The life he's never known.

SCENE THREE

~~~~~

COLIN'S ROOM

Archibald sits down beside Colin's bed, his shoulders casting a rounded shadow on the walls. He holds a book.

ARCHIBALD: Now, let's see . . .
  (Speaks)
  When we left off last night,
  The hideous dragon
  Had carried the maid to his cave by moonlight.
  He gnashed his teeth, breathed his fire,
  The heath quaked, and we trembled in fear.
  I said

  (Sings)
  Someone must save this
  Sweet raven-haired maiden,
  Though surely the cost will be steep.
  So we lads all drew lots,
  Our insides tied in knots,
  And I won and the rest went to sleep.

82

So I picked up my staff
And I followed the trail of
His smoke to the mouth of the cave.
And I bid him come out,
Yea forsooth, I did shout,
Ye fool dragon be gone or behave.

And then under my breath
I uttered a charm said
To make the worst fiend become kind—
Knaves and knights of dire plights
Now diminish his sights—
And it worked and the dragon went blind.

And he charged off the cliff
Howling mad and he died and the
Maiden accepted my ring.
And then you came along
And were brave, bold and strong,
And in thanks every night now I sing . . .

    Race you to the top of the morning,
    Come sit on my shoulders and ride.
    Run and hide, I'll come find you,
    Climb hills to remind you I love you,
    My boy at my side.

Now another foul dragon's
Appeared, I must leave you.
He's scorching our land with his breath.
From his lair, this one taunts me,
He dares me, he haunts me,
Once again, we must fight to the death.

Would to God I could stay and instead
Slay your dragon,
This beast who sits hunched on your back.
Would God I could wrench him
   Away from your bed,
Or cut off or tear off
   His terrible head,
Could breathe out my fire on him
   Till he was dead,
Or beg him to spare you
   And take me instead.

As it is, I must leave you
In care of my brother, the
Wizard who lives on the hill.
Who has promised his art
Will soon pierce through the heart
Of this dragon that's keeping you ill.

And I know that your mother,
God bless her, would want you
To do as he says and grow strong.
And you know that as soon as I can
I'll return, so be brave, son, and
Know that I long . . .

   To race you to the top of the morning,
   Come sit on my shoulders and ride.
   Run and hide, I'll come and find you,
   Climb hills to remind you I love you,
   I love you . . .
   My boy at my side.

Set design by Heidi Landesman for the 1991 Broadway production at the St. James Theatre. *Photo by Marc Bryan-Brown*

Rebecca Luker (left) as Lily with Mandy Patinkin as Archibald in the 1991 Broadway production. *Photo by Bob Marshak*

Daisy Eagan (left) as Mary with John Babcock as Colin in the 1991 Broadway production. *Photo by Bob Marshak*

John Cameron Mitchell as Dickon in the 1991 Broadway production. *Photo by Bob Marshak*

Archibald stands and exits.

Rose and Albert appear, as the scene changes to the garden.

ALBERT:
Miss a step, trip and fall,

ROSE:
Miss the path, meet the wall.

ALBERT:
Miss the way,

ROSE:
Miss a turn,

ALBERT AND ROSE:
Getting lost is how you learn.
It's a maze this garden, it's a maze of paths
Meant to lead a man astray.
Take a left and then turning left again's
How a soul may find the way . . .

SCENE FOUR

IN THE GREENHOUSE

Mary is seated on a bench in the greenhouse. Dickon enters.

DICKON: Ay op. Hello there, Mary.

MARY *(Clearly unhappy)*: Ay op. Hello there.

DICKON: But why are you in such a bad temper, Mary? Are ye
weary of lookin' for the key?

MARY: No, no. I found the key.

DICKON: You did?

She shows it to him.

DICKON: So I see. You're weary of lookin' for the door.

MARY: I'm not weary, Dickon. I found the door too. The garden
is dead.

DICKON: No.

MARY: It is. It's all dead.

DICKON: A lot of things what looks dead is just bidin' their time,
Mary. Now you tell me exactly what you saw.

MARY: It's cold and gray. The trees are gray, the earth is gray.
And there's this clingy kind of haze over everything.

86

DICKON: Like a body were in a dream.

MARY: It's the most forgotten place I've ever seen. With loose
gray branches looped all around the trees like ropes . . . or
snakes, and dead roots and leaves all tangled up on the
ground. So still and cold.

DICKON: But did you look real close at anything? Did you scrape
away a bit of the bark and have a real look at anything?
Mary. The strongest roses will fair thrive on bein' neglected,
if the soil is rich enough. They'll run all wild, and spread and
spread till they're a wonder.

MARY: You mean it might be alive? But how can we tell?

DICKON: Oh, I can tell if a thing is wick or not.

MARY (*Now truly excited*): Wick! I've heard Ben say wick.

DICKON:

When a thing is wick it has a life about it,
Maybe not a life like you and me.
But somewhere there's a secret streak of green inside it,
Now come and let me show you what I mean.

When a thing is wick it has a light around it,
Maybe not a light that you can see.
But hiding down below a spark's asleep inside it, just
Waiting for the right time to be seen.

You clear away the dead parts
So the tender buds can form,
Loosen up the earth and
Let the roots get warm,
Let the roots get warm.

When a thing is wick it has a way of knowing
When it's safe to grow again, you will see.

When there's sun and water sweet enough to feed it, it will
Climb up through the earth a pale new green.

> You clear away the dead parts
> So the tender buds can form,
> Loosen up the earth and
> Let the roots get warm,
> Let the roots get warm.

Come a mild day,
Come a warm rain,
Come a snowdrop a comin' up.
Come a lily,
Come a lilac,
Come to call,
Callin' all of us to come and see . . .

MARY:
> When a thing is wick,
> And someone cares about it,
> And comes to work each day,
> Like you and me,
> *(Spoken)*
> Will it grow?

DICKON: It will.

MARY:
> Then have no doubt about it,
> We'll have the grandest garden ever seen.
> *(Spoken)*

Oh, Dickon, I want it all to be wick! Would you come look
at it with me?

DICKON: I'll come every day, rain or shine, if you want me to.
All that garden needs is us to come wake it up.

MARY: But Dickon, what if we save the garden and then Uncle
Archie takes it back, or Colin wants it?

DICKON: Ay, what a miracle that would be. Gettin' a poor
crippled boy to see his mother's garden.

DICKON AND MARY:
You give a living thing
A little chance to grow,
That's how you will know if she is wick, she'll grow.

So grow to greet the morning,
Free from ground below,
When a thing is wick
It has a will to grow and grow.

MARY:
Come a mild day,
Come a warm rain,
Come a snowdrop a comin' up.
Come a lily,
Come a lilac,
Come to call,
Callin' all the rest to come . . .

DICKON AND MARY:
Callin' all of us to come,
Callin' all the world to come . . .

Dickon and Mary hear the chirp of the robin and quickly gather plants from the greenhouse and exit.

Alice appears.

ALICE:
So he picked up his staff
And he followed the trail of the smoke
To the mouth of the cave.
And he bid him come out,
Yea, forsooth, he did shout,
Ye fool dragon, begone or behave.

SCENE FIVE

COLIN'S ROOM

Colin is throwing a terrible tantrum. Martha and a Nurse are trying to calm him.

COLIN: Stop looking at me! I hate you! You're horrible and ugly, under that haystack you call your hair!

MARTHA: Master Colin, please. Nurse's only tryin' to—

COLIN: If she won't close her eyes when she's in my presence, then I will have her sent away. (*To the Nurse*) Go away! Go away! Go away!

MARTHA: Master Colin, please. Nurse's only tryin' to bring you your supper.

MRS. MEDLOCK (*Entering*): Martha! What is going on in here!

Mary enters.

MARY: Isn't anybody going to stop that boy?

MRS. MEDLOCK (*As she sees Mary*): She is *not* to go near him, Martha. Those are the doctor's direct orders.

MARTHA: What can it hurt, mum? He likes Mary. Let her have a go at it.

MRS. MEDLOCK: No, Martha.

And without waiting for approval, Mary runs over to the bed.

MARY: Colin Craven, you stop that screaming!
COLIN: Get away from me!
MARY: I hate you! Everybody hates you! You will scream yourself
to death in a minute and I wish you would!
COLIN: Get out of my house!
MARY: I won't! You stop!
COLIN: I can't stop! I felt a lump on my back. I'm going to die!
MARY: There is nothing the matter with your horrid back!
COLIN: I'm going to have a hunch on my back like my father
and die!
MARY: Martha! Come here and show me his back this minute.
MARTHA: I can't, Mary. He won't let me.
COLIN: Show her the lump!

Martha pulls aside Colin's covers and bedclothes.

COLIN: Now feel it!

Mary feels his back.

COLIN: There!
MARY: Where?
COLIN: Right there!
MARY: No! There's not a single lump there. Except backbone
lumps and they're supposed to be there. (*She turns her own
back to him*) See. I have them too.

*Mary grabs his hand and puts it on her back. And then places his hand on
his own back for comparison.*

MARY: See? There's no lump.

COLIN *(Quietly)*: It's not there.

MARY: No, it's not.

He sits up a little straighter. Looking slightly pleased.

COLIN: It's not there.

MARY: You were just mad at me for not coming back when I said I would.

He doesn't answer.

MARY: Weren't you.

COLIN: Maybe.

MARY *(Calmly)*: You were and you know it.

MARTHA: I'll leave you two alone, I think. *(She leaves)*

Mary opens a music box, determined not to speak to him until he apologizes.

MARY: This is nice.

Colin relents.

COLIN: I'm sorry I said all those things about sending Dickon away. I was just so angry when you wanted to be with him instead of me. And then when you didn't come back like you said you would—

MARY: I was always coming back, Colin. I'm as lonely as you are. I was just late, that's all. It just took me longer than I thought because . . . *(She stops)*

COLIN: Because what?

Mary takes a moment.

MARY: Will you promise not to tell if I tell you?

COLIN: I never had a secret before, except that I wasn't going to grow up.

MARY: I found your mother's garden.

COLIN: Do you mean a secret garden? I've dreamed about a secret garden.

MARY: It's been locked up out there, just like you've been locked up in here, for ten years. Because your father doesn't want anybody in it. Only I found the key. And the other night, after Dr. Craven and Mrs. Medlock found us here together, I ran out into the storm, and found the door. And now Dickon and I are working on it every day, and you can come too and—

COLIN: What does it look like?

MARY: Well, right now, there's this tangle of vines all over everything because nobody's been taking care of it, but Dickon says if we cut away all the dead wood, there'll be fountains of roses by summer.

COLIN: I never wanted to see anything like I want to see that garden.

MARY: You *must* see it. But they must never know where we're going or Ben says that Dr. Craven will send me away.

COLIN: No, Mary.

MARY (*Going on*): Maybe William can take you outside in your wheelchair, and leave us at the front steps. And then, when nobody's looking, Dickon could push you through the maze to the garden.

COLIN: I can't go outside, Mary. I'll take a chill if I go. I'll get even worse.

MARY: No you won't. You'll feel better.

A moment.

COLIN: I can't, Mary. I'm afraid.

And then Mary sees, in a shaft of light, the two officers who found her in India.

COLIN: I've been in this bed for so long. And I don't want to die.

LIEUTENANT WRIGHT: Just one blacksnake and this girl.

MAJOR HOLMES: I'm afraid there's no one left. Sorry, Miss.

Mary turns back to Colin.

COLIN: I want to grow up, Mary. So I can't get sick. *(He pauses)* I'd like to see the garden, really I would. But I can't.

Lieutenant Wright and Major Holmes exit.

MARY: All right, then. We'll just keep working on it till you're *ready* to see it. And whenever that is, you just tell me, and I'll get William to—

COLIN: You must come back tomorrow afternoon after you're through working, and have supper with me and tell me everything you've done.

MARY: I'd like that. Good night, then.

COLIN: Good night, Mary.

Mary leaves and as Colin looks out the window, Lily emerges from behind Colin's bed, and begins to sing.

LILY:
Come to my garden,
Nestled in the hill.

There I'll keep you
Safe beside me.

Come to my garden,
Rest there in my arms,
There I'll see you
Safely grown and on your way.

Stay there in my garden,
Where love grows free and wild.
Come to my garden,
Come, sweet child.

COLIN:

Lift me up and lead me to the garden,
Where life begins anew.
Where I'll find you,
And I'll find you love me too.

COLIN:

Lift me up,
And lead me to the garden,
Where love grows
   deep and true.
Where I'll tell you,
Where I'll show you,
My new life,
   I will live for you.

I shall see you
   in your garden,

LILY:

Come
To my garden,
Rest there
   in my arms.
There I'll
See you
Safely grown and
   on your way.

I shall see you
   in my garden,

And spring will
  come and stay.
Lift me up,
And lead me to the garden,
Come, sweet day.

Where love grows
  free and wild.
Come
To my garden,
Come, sweet day.

Lily embraces Colin and night closes in around them.

SCENE SIX

IN THE MAZE—THE GARDEN

By lantern light, Dickon and Martha are seen moving through the gardens.

MARTHA: Oh, I shouldn't be doin' this. I'm like to be sent back to the scullery for this, and I don't like the scullery, Dickon. I don't know anyone who does.

DICKON: No one'll be missin' you at this hour.

MARTHA: But if it's so dark I can't even see where I'm goin', how'm I to hope to see what it is once I get there?

DICKON: I can't say. Perhaps it's only somethin' you're meant to hear.

MARTHA: But all I can hear is my own self talkin'.

DICKON: Then perhaps, ye'd best be still.

Mary appears, pushing Colin in his wheelchair.

MARY: Dickon, is that you?

DICKON: Aye, it is, Mary. And Martha, too.

Martha is overcome, seeing Colin outside.

MARTHA: Oh dear lad.

COLIN: Martha, are you surprised to see me outside in the middle of the night?

MARTHA: That I am, Master Colin. But just now, you looked so much like your mother, it made my heart jump.

And with that, Dickon takes over from Mary and wheels Colin into . . .

THE NIGHT GARDEN

COLIN: It's my mother's garden. It is.

MARY: It's a secret garden. And we're the only ones in the world who want it to be alive.

DICKON: Ay, Colin. We'll have you walkin' about and diggin' same as other folk before long.

COLIN: But how can I? My legs are so weak, I'm afraid to—

DICKON: There's a charm in this garden, Colin. And the longer you stay in it, the stronger you'll be.

COLIN: What kind of a charm?

Suddenly, the Fakir and the Ayah appear, and Mary begins to intone an Indian-sounding charm.

MARY AND FAKIR:
A'o jadu ke mausam.
A'o garmiyo ke din.
A'o mantra tantra yantra
Us ki bimari hata 'o.

Colin stares at her in amazement.

COLIN: Where did you learn that?

MARY: I don't *know.* I didn't even know I *knew* it.

COLIN: Martha, do *you* believe in spells and charms?

MARTHA: That I do, Master Colin, and spirits and the Big Good Thing by whatever name you call it.

MARY (*As surprised as anyone by this*): Now I know where I heard it. I even know what it means.

COLIN: Go on, then.

MARY (*Speaking*):

    Come spirit, come charm,
    Come days that are warm,
    Come magical spell,
    Come help him get well.

DICKON (*Sings*):

    Come spirit, come charm,
    Come days that are warm,
    Come magical spell,
    Come help him get well.

Martha picks up the Yorkshire version and sings.

MARTHA:

    Come spirit, come charm,
    Come days that are warm,
    Come magical spell,
    Come help him get well.

And then the Fakir and the Ayah chant, as Martha and Dickon sing.

The Secret Garden

MARTHA AND DICKON:

Spirits all around,
Charms of earth, so near—

Tend the sleeping buds
Buried safely here,

Thaw the frozen ground,
Let the spring break through.
With spirits standing guard
Life will come . . . anew.

AYAH, FAKIR AND MARY:
A'o jadu ke
Mausam.

A'o garmiyo
Ke din.

Jadu ke
Mau-
Sam
A'o.

The Dreamers and Lily join in the singing, as Mary continues to weave her spell.

MARTHA, DICKON, LILY AND
  DREAMERS:
Spirits far above,
Charms aloft, on high—
Sweep away the storms
Rumbling 'cross the sky,
Speed the rising sun,
Make the breeze to blow,
Bid the robins sing,
Bid the roses grow.

MARY, AYAH, FAKIR:

A'o jadu ke
Mausam.
A'o garmiyo
Ke din mau-
Sam
Ke din
A'o.

And the dance begins, as Mary invites first Dickon, and then Martha, to join her. Finally, led by the Fakir and the Ayah, all the Dreamers are dancing with them, circling around the garden and Colin to work the spell of healing.

ALL:
>Come spirit, come charm,
>Come days that are warm,
>Come magical spell,
>Come help him get well.
>Come spirit, come charm.

And as they are all standing there, silent after the final moment of the round, Colin eases himself out of his wheelchair and stands.

COLIN: Mary, take my hand.

MARTHA: Oh, dear lad.

MARY: Colin. Look at you.

COLIN: I think the spell is working in the house too. *(A moment)* Two nights ago, when it was bright moonlight, I woke up and felt something filling the room and making everything so splendid. And I pulled the drape from my mother's picture, and there she was, her eyes looking right down at me, and something new started flooding through me, making me so proud, so strong . . . so . . . tall. *(A moment)* I shall live forever and ever! I shall find out thousands of things. *(He takes another step)* I want to give thanks to something, to anything that will listen. *(And another step)* I'm well!

MARTHA: Mary, child, do you see what you've done?

But as Mary helps Colin take a few steps, he is distracted by the sight of something, and falls.

COLIN: Who is that man? Go away!

Mary and Dickon help Colin back into his chair.

MARY: Colin, it's Ben Weatherstaff, who tends the gardens.

COLIN: Weatherstaff! Do you know who I am?

Ben approaches.

BEN: You're young Master Colin, the poor cripple, but Lord knows how you got out here.

COLIN: I'm not crippled!

BEN: Then what have you been doing, hidin' out and lettin' folk *think* you were a cripple. And half-witted!

COLIN: Half-witted!

Mary laughs, and Colin gives her a stern look.

COLIN: Come here. I want to talk to you. And don't you dare say a word about this.

BEN: I'm your servant, as long as I live, young master.

COLIN: Did you know my mother?

BEN: That I did. I was her right-hand, round the gardens. Even now, I'm only kept on because she liked me. She said to me once, Ben, if I'm ever ill or if I go away, you must take care of my roses. (*A moment*) When she did go away, the orders was no one was to come in here. But I come anyway, till my back stopped me, about two year ago.

COLIN: I want to know how she died.

BEN (*After a moment*): She was sittin' right there, on that branch. And it broke and that started her laborin' with you, only the fall had hurt her back. Still she clung onto life till you were born and then she put you in your father's arms and died.

COLIN: Is that why he hates me?

BEN: I'm sure he doesn't hate you, lad.

MARY: He doesn't even know you. Wait till he finds out you can stand.

COLIN: I don't want him to know anything about this. I don't want anything said to him till I can walk. Do you promise?

BEN: It's gettin' to be a full-time job, keepin' track of all the secrets around here.

COLIN: This is a serious matter. Mary. Take my hand. Dickon. Martha. You too, Ben.

They form a circle around him.

COLIN: Do you swear by the charm in this garden, that not one of you will mention this to my father until I am completely well?

They swear. More or less in unison.

BEN: That I do.

DICKON: Ay, Colin. Nary a word.

MARTHA: Ay, Colin.

MARY: I promise.

COLIN: Good, then.

He releases their hands.

MARY: So what do you want to see first?

COLIN: I want to see the roses. Show me where the roses will be.

As they go off to look at the roses, Albert, Lily and Rose appear.

LILY, ROSE AND ALBERT:
A bit of earth,
A drop of dew, a single stem,

Begins to rise.
That bit of earth
Is pushed aside, the flowers bloom
Before our eyes.

For in the earth
A charm's at work, the word is
Passed, the days are warm,
Unfold and grow,
The winter's past,
We're free from harm.

A bit of earth
A bit of earth . . .

SCENE SEVEN

THE LIBRARY

Dr. Craven and Mrs. Medlock are in the library awaiting the arrival of the headmistress from the school they have selected for Mary. Dr. Craven is in an uncharacteristically good humor.

DR. CRAVEN: Well, Mrs. Medlock. What a fine morning this has turned out to be.

MRS. MEDLOCK: Yes, doctor.

DR. CRAVEN: I trust this headmistress will be quite impressed, riding 'cross the moor on such a day. Perhaps she could even join me for lunch. I daresay she might relish a bit of civilized conversation, living as she does, in the company of spinsters and orphaned girls.

Mrs. Medlock is somewhat offended by that remark.

MRS. MEDLOCK: I'm sure she would be quite flattered by your attention, sir.

Jane, a housemaid, appears with Mrs. Winthrop.

JANE: Beg pardon, doctor. It's Mrs. Winthrop, sir.

Jane exits.

DR. CRAVEN: Yes, madam. Come in. Do come in. Please. And this is our housekeeper, Mrs. Medlock.

MRS. WINTHROP: How do you do.

DR. CRAVEN: I trust you had a pleasant journey.

MRS. WINTHROP: Actually, not, doctor. I have always found scenery, by itself, to be quite tiresome.

DR. CRAVEN: Well, then, you will be relieved to find we have contrived to keep all the scenery outdoors. Won't you sit down. (*Taking the forms from his jacket*) I've completed all the forms you sent us, and I think you'll see my brother has included a contribution to the school's building fund. You didn't request it, of course, but as I told my brother, I'm sure you're in the planning stages of something or other. Mrs. Medlock, will you see what's keeping Mary.

MARY: I'm right here, sir.

Mary enters, followed by the Fakir and the Ayah.

DR. CRAVEN: Quite right. Here's our girl. Mary Lennox, this is Mrs. Winthrop, of the Aberdeen School for Girls.

MRS. WINTHROP: Good morning, Mary.

MARY: I don't want to go to a school.

MRS. WINTHROP: Oh, but you do. A useless child never knows her worth, we say.

MARY: My Uncle Archibald said—

DR. CRAVEN: Perhaps if you would tell Mary a little about the school, she'd see there is no reason to be—

MRS. WINTHROP: Certainly. And let me say from the start that you are not on trial here. The board of directors has accepted your application.

DR. CRAVEN: That's good news, indeed.

MARY: I won't go. You can't make me.

Mary throws a cookie on the floor.

DR. CRAVEN: Mary Lennox!

MRS. WINTHROP: That's all right, doctor. This is exactly the type of behavior we are best equipped to handle.

MARY: My Uncle Archibald is the only one who says where I'm going to go and he says I don't have to go to any stupid school!

DR. CRAVEN: She's just frightened, I'm sure. Children are quite often depressed after a tragedy such as she has suffered.

MRS. WINTHROP: Of course, doctor. Thank you. Perhaps she would enjoy seeing some photographs of the girls at their work. I've brought several samples of the fine lace for which our girls are so—

Mrs. Winthrop forces Mary to pick up the cookie.

MARY: I hate you! You're a horrible, ugly pig.

DR. CRAVEN: That's quite enough, young lady!

MARY: Your school is a filthy rathole full of brats and dirty beds. And all anybody really does there is scrub floors! I hope you get hit by a lorry on the way home and your ugly head rolls off in a ditch and gets eaten by maggots! I hate you! I hate you! I hate you! And if I'm sent off with you, I'm going to bite your arm and you're going to die! Get out of here!

She throws a chair.

MARY: Go away! Go away! Go away!

MRS. WINTHROP: Well, we have had one or two cases of this severity.

Mary stamps on Mrs. Winthrop's foot.

DR. CRAVEN: Mary Lennox!

Mary launches into a full-blown tantrum, cursing in Hindi as the Ayah and the Fakir make menacing voodoo signs and native droning sounds upstage.

MARY:

Mar jaa>o!	(Die!
Mar jaa>o!	Die!
Baarh me jaa>o!	Go drown yourself in the flood!
Chhoro mujhe!	Leave me alone!
Tum barii shaitaan ho!	You're a big devil!
Mar jaa>o!	Die!)

Mary finishes by whirling around and falling to the floor, feigning unconsciousness.

Mrs. Winthrop picks up her purse and papers.

MRS. WINTHROP: Dr. Craven, what you have here, is a medical problem.

Mrs. Winthrop exits. Mary feels quite proud of herself. Dr. Craven looks down at her.

DR. CRAVEN: I'll speak with Mary alone, Medlock.

Mary gets up and curses him again.

MARY: Chhoro mujhe! I'm going outside.

DR. CRAVEN (*Grabbing her*): You're going wherever I send you, young lady, and right this moment it's into that chair.

MARY: Uncle Archibald said I didn't have to go to a school.

DR. CRAVEN: Oh for God's sake. He doesn't care about you. All he wants is never to see you again. Why do you think he left without even saying good-bye to you?

MARY: Maybe he was in a hurry.

DR. CRAVEN: You drove him away. You remind him of his wife.

MARY: I look like my Aunt Lily?

DR. CRAVEN: Now it is my task to find you a suitable place to go so that *he* can return. The other school I have contacted will send no representative. Your bags will be packed and you will leave Saturday week.

MARY: But I can't leave now. Colin needs me.

DR. CRAVEN: The last thing the boy needs is you. Another month of trying to keep up with you and we'll have to put him in hospital, or worse.

MARY: No you won't. He's much better.

DR. CRAVEN: You have no idea how sick he is. When Colin was born, the midwife didn't expect him to live a week. But I have kept the boy alive for ten years. Only now, thanks to you, he is in grave danger of relapse.

MARY: But you haven't seen how—

DR. CRAVEN: Do you want him in hospital? Do you want him to die?

MARY: To die?

DR. CRAVEN: Yes! To die. If Colin is too active at this stage in his recovery, if you push him to take his first step too soon, before his heart is strong enough, he will not survive it. Do you understand, Mary? Colin's very life is in your hands.

Suddenly, Lieutenant Wright and Major Holmes appear.

DR. CRAVEN: One moment, he would be chatting away, and the
next moment, he would sink to the ground and die.

MARY: And die?

DR. CRAVEN: Yes! You *have* choices in your life. Colin does not.
I will not see the boy in hospital for the rest of his life, or
dead before his life even begins. You must go, and go you
will. Now that is all I have to say to you.

Mary cannot answer. But she doesn't leave.

DR. CRAVEN: Why are you standing here? Are you quite amused
to learn of your power?

MARY: I didn't do anything. You locked him in his room.

DR. CRAVEN: You may go.

MARY: You don't want Colin to get well at all. You want him to
die so you can have this house.

*Suddenly almost out of control, Dr. Craven raises his arm, as though to
hit Mary. Then he stops himself.*

DR. CRAVEN *(Screaming)*: You will leave Saturday week!

Mary runs from the room, and Dr. Craven sings.

DR. CRAVEN:
There's nothing here that I want.
How dare she make this claim?
Isn't it clear what I want?
To serve has been my aim.

Still, I have to wonder
Who I'd be,
If it all belonged to me.

If they'd all disappear
I'd start again.
I could be happy then,
I'd live like other men.

If they'd all disappear
I could be free.
Cut off from pain and loss
At last, I'd be.

SCENE EIGHT

⟿⟦❀⟧⟿

MARY'S ROOM

As Martha packs some of Mary's clothes, she tries to comfort the girl.

MARTHA: You had *nothing* to do with your uncle's leaving. It
weren't you, child. Your uncle liked you, I know he did.
Didn't he tell you you could have a garden? Didn't he send
you clothes and bring you books? Well, didn't he?

MARY: But Colin's going to die and it's all my fault.

MARTHA: And what have you done for Colin except get him
goin' outside every day, and get him eatin' his food and gettin'
him believin' he can get strong again? I think you were just
what Colin needed.

MARY: But you're not a doctor, Martha. Will you tell him I'm
sorry. I mean, after I'm gone, will you tell him I didn't mean
to hurt him, that I didn't want to go?

MARTHA: I think you better tell him that yourself.

MARY: I can't, Martha. He'll just get mad and start acting all
high and mighty. And then Dr. Craven might send him
away, too.

MARTHA: You're talkin' like you're already gone, Mary Lennox.

MARY: I *am* gone, Martha. I wish I were a ghost.

MARTHA: No ghost could do what you've done in this house,
Mary.
(*Sings*)
What you've got to do is
Finish what you have begun.
I don't know just how, but
It's not over till you've won.

When you see the storm is comin',
See the lightning part the skies,
It's too late to run,
There's terror in your eyes.
What you do then is remember
This old thing you heard me say —
It's this storm, not you,
That's bound to blow away.

    Hold on,
    Hold on to someone standin' by.
    Hold on,
    Don't even ask how long or why.
    Child, hold on to what you know is true,
    Hold on till you get through.
    Child oh child,
    Hold on.

When you feel your heart is poundin',
Fear a devil's at your door,
There's no place to hide,
You're frozen to the floor.

What you do then is you force yourself
To wake up and you say—
It's this dream not me
That's bound to go away.

Hold on,
Hold on the night will soon be by.
Hold on,
Until there's nothin' left to try.
Child, hold on, there's angels on their way.
Hold on and hear them say—
Child oh child . . .

And it doesn't even matter if
The danger and the doom
Come from up above, or down below,
Or just come flyin' at you
From across the room . . .

When you see a man who's ragin',
And he's jealous and he fears
That you've walked through walls
He's hid behind for years,
What you do then is you tell yourself
To wait it out, you say—
It's this day, not me, that's
Bound to go away.

Child, hold on,
It's this day, not you
That's bound to go away.

MARY: What do you think I should do?

MARTHA: I think you should find a pen and paper and write to your uncle in Paris and tell him to come home. I think you should let Colin's father say whether he likes him standin' or not.

MARY: But why would he listen to me? And what if the letter didn't get to him in time?

MARTHA: I'm sure your uncle will send for you as soon as he sees what you've done for the boy. (*Getting the paper*) Now here's some paper, and here's a pen. You do know how to write, I hope. 'Cause I won't be much help to you in that department.

MARY: A little.

MARTHA: That's all right. You don't have *much* to say, do you.

Mary begins to write.

MARTHA (*Sings*):
  D-E-A-R . . .

MARY (*Sings*):
  . . . Uncle Archie,

Far upstage, Archibald appears in Paris, reading the letter.

MARY:
  How are you, I'm fine.
  Everybody else is too.
  Please come home.

ARCHIBALD: Home, I have no home.

MARY:

Martha says you're in Paris.
Is that very far away?

ARCHIBALD: It's a house, child. Just a house.

MARY:

Do they have nice girls and boys there?
Please come home.

ARCHIBALD: And I can't get far enough away from it.
MARTHA: Now just sign it . . .

But Mary turns to Martha, wondering what else she should put in the letter.

MARY:

Should I say that Colin's well now?

ARCHIBALD (*Sings*):

Streets of Paris like a maze . . .

MARY:

Should I say that Dr. Craven . . .

ARCHIBALD:

Sleepless nights and aimless days . . .

MARTHA:

I think that what you have is good.
Let's get it posted, on its way.
He'll rush home, then you can tell
Him all the rest you have to say.

MARY:
Oh kind sir,
Uncle Archie,
How I wish that
    you could see . . .
When you come
    into the garden . . .
Please, come home . . .

Yours truly?

ARCHIBALD:

Can't forget,
Can't eat or sleep
    or live . . .

Can't forgive . . .

MARTHA: Well, maybe . . .

MARY:
    Sincerely?

MARTHA: Well, how about . . .

MARY:
    Your friend, Mary.

Martha and Mary go offstage as Archibald sings.

SCENE NINE

PARIS

ARCHIBALD:

  Now I see you in the window
  Of a carriage, then a train,
  Still my mind will not accept that
  In your grave you must remain.
  I hear your voice, then turn and
  See a stranger's form and face.
  Must I wander on tormented
  Place to place to place to place.

  Where can I go that you won't find me?
  Why can't I find a place to hide?
  Why do you want to chase me, haunt me,
  Every step you're there beside me?

  Where in the world, tell me where in the world
    Can I live without your love?
  Where on the earth, tell me where on the earth
    Can I stay now that you are gone.

Why did I have to meet you, love you,
Why can't I rid you from my mind?
Why did you have to want me, won't you
Let me put my life behind me?

How in the world, tell me how in the world
  Can I live without your love?
Why on the earth, tell me why on the earth
  Should I stay now that you are gone?
Now . . . that you are—

Suddenly, Lily appears behind him.

ARCHIBALD (*Speaks*): Lily? Is that you?

LILY:

How could I know I would have to leave you,
How could I know I would hurt you so?
You were the one I was born to love.
Oh, how . . . could I ever know,
How could I ever know?

How can I say to go on without me,
How when I know you still need me so?
How can I say not to dream about me?
How could I ever know,
How could I ever know.

Forgive me,
Can you forgive me?
And hold me in your heart,
And find some new way to love me,

Now that we're apart . . .

She approaches him, and finally moves to touch him, her hands embracing his shoulders.

LILY:
How could I know I would never hold you,
Never again in this world, but oh,
Sure as you breathe, I am there inside you.
How . . . could I ever know,
How could I ever know.

He turns to sing directly to her.

ARCHIBALD:
How can I hope to go on without you,
How can I know where you'd have me go?
How can I bear not to dream about you?
How can I let you go?

LILY:
How could I ever know.

The music picks up the melody from the waltz in the first act.

ARCHIBALD:
All I need is . . .

LILY:
. . . is there in the garden.

ARCHIBALD:
All I would ask is . . .

LILY:

. . . is care for the child of

LILY AND ARCHIBALD:

. . . our love.

LILY:

Come, go with me,
Safe I will keep you,

ARCHIBALD:

Where you would lead me,
There I would,

LILY:

There I would, there we would,

LILY AND ARCHIBALD:

There we will go . . .

How, how could I know,
Tell me, how, how could I know,
Ever to know you will never leave me . . .
How could we ever know,
How could we know.

ARCHIBALD:

How could I ever know?

LILY:

Come to my garden . . .

Lily takes Archibald by the hand and leads him back to the garden.

SCENE TEN

❧

THE DAY GARDEN

It is morning in the garden. Voices are heard from offstage.

COLIN: Mary! What is it?

Dickon and Martha appear.

DICKON: Mary! Come quickly!
MARY: Wait till you see it!

Mary wheels Colin into the garden.

COLIN: Mary, what is it?
MARY: It's spring!
COLIN: But where did it come from?
DICKON: From all our hard work, where do you think?
COLIN: Everything is so . . . . Look at it!
MARY: But where's Ben? He has to see what's happened.
MARTHA: I'll go and fetch him.

Martha exits to look for Ben.

DICKON: Colin, look at the lilacs . . .

Dickon wheels Colin round and round in the wheelchair.

DICKON *(Sings):*
  Come spirit, come charm,
  Come days that are warm,
  Come gather and sing
  And welcome the spring.

MARY, DICKON AND COLIN:
  Come, come spirit,
  Come charm,
  Come gather and sing
  And welcome the spring.

COLIN: Mary, look at the roses!
MARY: There *are* fountains of them!
COLIN *(Speaks):*
  Mistress Mary, quite contrary,
  How does your garden grow . . .

Mary grabs Dickon's staff and taunts Colin in return.

MARY: I'm not contrary. You take that back.
COLIN: You make me!

Dickon wheels Colin offstage, chased by Mary.

MARY: I will! I've got you, Colin Craven!

And suddenly, Lily leads Archibald and Dr. Craven into the garden.

DR. CRAVEN: Archie, why didn't you cable us you were coming?

ARCHIBALD: I didn't know myself, Neville.

Dr. Craven hears Mary shrieking with delight.

DR. CRAVEN: What on earth is all that noise!

COLIN (*Unseen*): Oh no you don't. I'm lots faster than you. Here we come!

Colin pushes Mary, now in the wheelchair, into view.

MARY: Colin Craven, not so fast!

DR. CRAVEN: Mary Lennox!

Colin stops as he sees his father and Dr. Craven.

COLIN: Father!

Archibald can't believe what he sees.

COLIN: Look at me! (*Crosses slowly to his father*) I'm well!

Archibald clasps the boy to him.

ARCHIBALD: Oh, Colin, my fine brave boy. Can you ever forgive me?

COLIN: It was the garden that did it, Father, and Mary and Dickon, and some kind of . . . charm that came right out of the ground.

ARCHIBALD: Neville, were you hoping to surprise me with this news?

DR. CRAVEN: I knew they were looking better, but I had no idea they were—

COLIN: We didn't want you to know. We were afraid you wouldn't let us come to the garden if you knew.

DR. CRAVEN: But how did you—

COLIN: William carried me down the stairs until—

DR. CRAVEN: But what have you eaten? You haven't touched the food we've sent to your rooms for weeks.

COLIN: Martha sent us food, and we ate in the garden. We ate enough for ten children.

ARCHIBALD: You did, did you.

COLIN: Oatcakes and roasted eggs and fresh milk and—

DR. CRAVEN: It was all terribly confusing. After all these years, to . . .

ARCHIBALD: It was confusing, Neville. Why don't you take my flat in Paris and stay as long as you like. And when you return, perhaps you will allow me to help you reestablish your practice, in town if you like, so you can resume your own life, free of the enormous burden you have carried on our behalf.

DR. CRAVEN: Thank you, Archie.

MARY (*To Archibald*): And will you stay home with us?

ARCHIBALD: Colin, Colin. Look at you.

COLIN: It was Ben that kept the garden alive, Father, until we could get here.

BEN: I knew it was against your orders, sir, but—

ARCHIBALD: As I remember, it was Lily who ordered you to take care of this garden, Ben. Well done.

BEN: Thank you, sir.

COLIN: And it was Dickon who taught us—

ARCHIBALD: Yes. I can imagine. Dickon, if there is ever anything we can do—

Martha interrupts him.

MARTHA: Sir. What is to become of our Mary?

ALBERT (*Sings*):
Clusters of crocus . . .

ARCHIBALD: Why, Mary.

MARY: Here's your key, if you want it back, sir. You didn't bury it after all. I'd have never found it if you—

ARCHIBALD: I had nearly forgotten you in all this.

MARY (*Bravely*): It's hard to remember everybody, sir.

ARCHIBALD: No it isn't. Three isn't very many people at all. I should be able to remember three people quite easily.

MARY (*Carefully*): Would I be one of them?

ARCHIBALD: Mary Lennox, for as long as you will have us, . . . we are yours, Colin and I, . . . and this is your home, and this, my lovely child . . . is your garden.

Mary rushes into his embrace and he holds her close as Colin and Martha clasp hands. The Dreamers approach, singing, then take their leave of Mary, one by one.

DREAMERS:
Come to my garden,
Nestled in the hill.
There I'll keep you safe
Beside me . . .
Come to my garden,
Rest there in my arms,
There I'll see you
Safely grown and on your way . . .

LILY, ROSE AND ALBERT:
Stay here in the garden
As days grow long and mild . . .

Rose and Albert exit.

Mary and Colin stand, with Archibald kneeling between them, as Lily sings.

LILY:
Come to the garden,
Come, sweet child.

She blows them a final kiss, walks upstage toward a garden path. We hear a single glissando and she disappears.

THE END